how come i feel so
disconnected

if this is such a user-friendly world?

RECONNECTING
WITH YOUR FAMILY, YOUR FRIENDS
... AND YOUR LIFE

marcia byalick and linda saslow

Peterson's

Princeton, New Jersey

to Mona and Marty—
who built the strong bridges
on which we base
our most enduring connections

Copyright © 1995 by Marcia Byalick and Linda Saslow

Library of Congress Cataloging-in-Publication Data
Byalick, Marcia, 1947–
    How come I feel so disconnected if this is such a user-friendly world: reconnecting with your family, your friends . . . and your life / Marcia Byalick and Linda Saslow
    p. cm.
    ISBN 1-56079-395-3
    1. Social networks—United States.   2. Social interaction—United States. 3. Interpersonal relations—United States.   4. Self-actualization (Psychology) I. Saslow, Linda, 1951– .   II. Title.   ,
    HM131.B93 1955   94-44125
    158′.2—dc 20   CIP

Cover and Interior Design by Kathy Kikkert

Printed in the United States of America

10 9 8 7 6 5 4 3 2 1

Acknowledgments

The best chroniclers are, in fact, a reflection of their sources of information and inspiration. Without the experts whom we tracked down across the country and our many friends, neighbors, and colleagues (and their friends, and friends of their friends . . .) we would never have been able to complete this project.

Our thanks to those who contributed their wisdom and wit and who helped us answer the question: How come we feel so disconnected if this is such a user-friendly world?

From ProfNet and the guidance of our local contacts at SUNY at Stony Brook, Dan Forbush and Vicki Katz: Dr. Timothy H. Brubaker, Miami University, Oxford, Ohio; Dr. Karen E. Campbell, Vanderbilt University; Dr. Theodore Caplow, University of Virginia; Dr. Dominick Cavallo, Adelphi University; Dr. Paul Ciborowski, Long Island University; Dr. Thomas Finholt, University of Michigan; Dr. Blair Justice, University of Texas; Dr. Joe Malloy, Hamilton College; Dr. Larry McCallum, Augustana College; Dr. Steven L. Nock, University of Virginia; Dr. Harry Reis, University of Rochester; Dr. William Vitek, Clarkson University; Dr. Barry Wellman, University of Toronto; Dr. Lynn White, University of Nebraska–Lincoln; and Dr. Meg Wilkes Karraker, University of St. Thomas.

From the worlds outside academia: Dr. Sallyann Amdur-Sack, psychologist, Bethesda, Maryland; Dr. Gilda Carle, communications specialist, Yonkers, New York; Rabbi Darryl Crystal, North Shore Synagogue, Syosset, New York; Dr. Bruce Ettenberg, technology coordinator, New York City; Jennifer Fahey, director of health and healing at Canyon Ranch, Lenox, Massachusetts; Norman Greenspan, assistant principal at Southwoods Middle School, Syosset, New York; Monsignor Thomas Hartman, director of radio and television for Diocesan Television Center,

Long Island, New York; Dr. Raymond Havlichek, director of the Institute of Psychosomatic Research, Roslyn, New York; Alice Hellerstein, genealogist, Rockville, Maryland; Abby Kenigsberg, executive director of the Long Island Coalition for Fair Broadcasting; Dr. Paul Lichtenberg, psychologist and poet, New York City; Rabbi David Nesenoff, Oyster Bay Jewish Center, Oyster Bay, New York; Dr. Michael Peltzman, psychologist, Roslyn, New York; Carl Pratt, spa director at Canyon Ranch, Lenox, Massachusetts; Frank H. T. Rhodes, president of Cornell University; Dr. Jeffrey Rossman, director of behavioral health at Canyon Ranch, Lenox, Massachusetts; Father James Royce, Seattle University; Dr. Jorge Schneider, principal of Syosset High School, Syosset, New York; Rabbi Arthur Schwartz, Kehillath Shalom, Cold Spring Harbor, New York; Al Splete, president of the Council of Independent Colleges; Families and Work Institute; United Way of Long Island; The Church of Jesus Christ of Latter-Day Saints; and The New Center for Wholistic Health, Education and Research, Syosset, New York.

And individually: our editor, Carol Hupping, who consistently improved our work with her suggestions and ideas; Abner Bergman, rabbi of Temple Judea in Manhasset, New York, and human connector extraordinaire, whose sermons and temple writings illuminated our research and nourished our souls; our friends, with whom we share a past full of cherished memories and dreams of a future with lots more time for hugs and laughs; our children, Jennifer and Carrie, Julie and Craig, on whom we practiced our rooting and bonding skills, and who in return taught us the rewards of unconditional love; and Bob and Jerry, our anchors, our partners, our ultimate connection.

Contents

vi

Introduction

If someone were to pay you one dollar for every time this year you found life rich enough in moments shared with those who mean the most to you, and you would have to give back fifty cents for every time you felt a bit detached, a smidgen displaced, or a tad disconnected—would you be rich or poor? If you're like us, the bad news is that we're not going to be dining on lobster any time soon. The good news is that there are plenty of ways available to generate more income.

One of us is a journalist who reports on issues concerning the health, education, and social welfare of her suburban community for a daily newspaper. The other is an essayist who writes on how the facts and statistics we read personally impact on the American family. Both of us, in our own work, spend many hours talking—and listening—to friends, neighbors, colleagues, even strangers who are willing and often eager to share their thoughts, feelings, and positions on topics both global and personal.

Over and over again we hear about the ultimate frustration of time crunches—the constant struggle of having to fit 30 hours worth of responsibilities, commitments and obligations into only 24. We hear about no time to nurture relationships with friends, neighbors, even family . . . and self.

We hear about a yearning to be part of the neighborhoods and communities of our childhood, an uneasiness in accepting the changes that are going on in the workplace, a skepticism that the

how come i feel so disconnected
if this is such a user-friendly world?

2

computer age can really supply us with the tools to reach out to others in satisfying, meaningful ways. Overall, we're sensing that an awful lot of people are feeling more than a tinge of discomfort with their lives.

We're also feeling it ourselves. Constantly trying to juggle the personal and professional roles of wife, mother, daughter, friend, neighbor, and writer, we're often overwhelmed by the never-ending demands in our daily lives. And we're frustrated by having to put too many important relationships on the back burner because our time is filled with trying to complete the items on our "must do" lists.

With the lifetime anchors of our own memory—neighbors, bosses, clergy, friends, even baseball teams—becoming a less reliable safety net in times of insecurity and isolation, we looked for ways to buttress and enhance them . . . and, if necessary, replace them. In our continued search, validated and reinforced by ongoing dialogue with those around us, we became convinced that collaborating on this project would be an exciting, worthwhile, and helpful adventure. Our task was to offer practical advice to help you find, build, and maintain stable and enduring connecting points in your life.

We hardly pretend to be experts in fields of psychology, sociology, theology, technology, communication, and business. But, as experienced chroniclers, we've talked to learned people in all these fields, and we share their insights with you to reassure you that we're all in this together and to inspire and motivate you to make some changes to reconnect with the people, places, and things most important in your life.

As we ourselves attempt to practice what we preach and learn to love not so much what we've acquired but what we have made and with whom we have made it, we see why it's so difficult. Many people, in a quest to keep up with the '90s, have lost a sense of purpose. We were raised to value self-sufficiency and independence— but what are they worth if they weaken the relationships and institutions we count on?

It's not that people today are shallow. Just ask—and most will answer that they want connections that go deeper than the usual interactions they have in today's society. The challenge is how to implement those meaningful connections—and to stay connected. The suggestions we offer flow across old borders and boundaries.

By presenting what we hope is a unique blend of suggestions, strategies, and practical advice, we will explore how you can improve your relationships with your family, friends, and neighbors; how to connect more successfully in the workplace; how to incorporate the customs and traditions of your religious heritage with the high-tech world of instant gratification; how to heighten your sense of belonging.

In our search for the most up-to-date information, we became living proof of our own message. Thanks to a service known as ProfNet, we were able to connect high-technically, via the Internet, with college campuses, universities, industrial research laboratories, and government-sponsored scientific institutions across the country, where we "talked" with experts in various fields—via phone, fax, and

how come i feel so disconnected
if this is such a user-friendly world?

4

e-mail—and were able to learn about the most recent research, review important studies, and receive first-hand professional suggestions and advice.

The personal perspective came to us, by phone, fax, mail, and face-to-face interviews, from many people gracious enough to share their own conflict and success stories. Our quest began with a questionnaire that we sent to over a hundred people, which was supplemented with dozens of phone calls and interviews. During the research process, our own personal buzzword became "serendipity"— some of the greatest stories, most inspiring anecdotes, absolutely best material fell into our laps when we weren't even looking for it.

We've read the depressing statistics describing a self-absorbed, cellularized America careening off into cyberspace. But we don't buy it. As women working hard to fulfill our multiple roles, we're convinced that although times may change, traditions and principles, character and human nature do not. If your ties are feeling more tenuous than you'd like, there are ways to redirect your energies away from self-fulfillment and refocus toward community. If those you feel closest to are too far away to share a porch or a stoop, what better time in history than right now to find alternative ways to instantly communicate? And if the dragon keeping you from bonding more successfully is lack of energy or money or nerve . . . it's time to slay him.

You get the picture; read on.

chapter one

"How Can I Be in My House and Feel So Far From Home?"

Reinventing the American Dream—Past, Present, and Personal

"We didn't all come over on the same ship, but we're all in the same boat."
—Bernard Baruch

how come i feel so disconnected
if this is such a user-friendly world?

6

Call me. Beep me. Page me. Fax me. Keep in touch. Stay close. Let me know where I can reach you. We've masterfully arranged to have our need to stay connected instantly gratified. We can talk to each other day and night—on a plane, in the bathroom, at the movies—yet what we're saying is somehow not doing the trick. For a nation obsessed with staying connected, too often many of us are feeling emotionally detached. It's like we've come down with a case of the blahs. No matter how many significant others we're attached to, how consuming our jobs, how demanding our responsibilities, a nagging sense of displacement appears to have pervaded the land. Too often useful relationships and meaningful encounters substitute for honest friendships.

But deep down we know that maintaining sincere human connections is key to our pursuit of happiness. What we need more than a quicker way to get there is companionship for the journey.

We can learn by looking at California's magnificent sequoias. These mighty trees, some as tall as skyscrapers, have roots practically at surface level. A lone sequoia can hardly stand up to a strong breeze, its roots are so shallow. So how do they grow so tall? Sequoias spring up in groves and their roots intertwine. They hold each other up. They give each other the strength necessary to withstand the angriest winds.

It works the same for us. Life's too hard to make it alone. It's through alliances grounded in support, encouragement, and acceptance that we grow strong. Together we can gather the energy needed to withstand almost anything life hurls our way.

People walk down the street with sunglasses and walkmans—pros at keeping others from knowing what they're hearing, watching, and thinking. You can sit down next to a woman on the bus who takes ten minutes to put on a full face of makeup every morning on the way to work—an intensely personal ritual—and she won't have a clue as to what you look like because she'll never even look your way. A father will make it his business to attend his son's Little League game but will have his ear attached to his office by cellular phone, disengaging his mind and body and utterly neutralizing his spirit. So absorbed do we sometimes become in the enterprise of being ourselves that we ignore the true source of our attitudes and emotions: our human bonds.

There's a story of a woman who received a gorgeous opal necklace as a wedding present. She decided she would wear it only on very, very special occasions. The years that followed presented many opportunities but she found none of them important enough. The necklace remained in the vault.

Many years later, the woman's daughter was getting married. With excitement and pride, she went to the vault, took out the box containing the necklace, and asked her daughter to open it. As she pulled the necklace from its case, the opals crumbled in the girl's hands. The woman was stunned. She didn't know that opals need to

> "The worst sin towards our fellow creatures is not to hate them, but to be indifferent to them; that's the essence of inhumanity."
> —George Bernard Shaw

how come i feel so disconnected
if this is such a user-friendly world?

8

be worn—that they need the oils of the skin in order to retain their luster and their strength. It is the warmth of the human body—the touching, the regular using—that gives them life.

People, too, need the touching of other people—the warmth, caring, and nurturing of each other—to grow in strength and luster of character. None of us ever becomes a successful "I" without a succession of "Thous" helping to make it possible.

This book points out ways—simple, free, and nonfattening—that all of us can improve the state of our union with our most important relationships. As in the case of the opals, knowing we possess them is not enough . . . we must be comfortable enough to appreciate them each and every day. At home and at work, with our friends and our neighbors, utilizing our religion and our computers, there are opportunities available to make us feel more in synch and less out of touch. What we do is mainly determined by what we believe. And if you believe your friendships might be languishing, your marriage growing numb, your work . . . just work, and/or your spiritual life lacking soul—the authors of this book believe we have some suggestions that can help.

> *"A hundred times every day I remind myself that my inner and outer life depend on the labours of other men, living and dead, and that I must exert myself in order to give in the same measure as I have received."*
> —*Albert Einstein*

• HOW DID WE GET HERE?

Before tackling new strategies, however, we should better understand why people feel the way they do. More than 100 years ago, Karl Marx studied workers who had just been introduced to one of the benefits of industrialization: the division of labor. He found that instead of benefiting from the changes, the workers suffered from a new disability: alienation. The more powerless they felt, the more estranged they became—from their work and themselves. Recent headlines echo his observations as too many of us suffer from the '90s version of the malady he describes.

> "Knowledge of what is possible is the beginning of happiness."
> —George Santayana

Today we are often described as "a society of strangers," "a generation of individualists," by the same social scientists who tell us that, on average, we have about 1,500 relationships with people we recognize by name and respond to one-on-one.[1] Why then, with so many people around us, do we feel disconnected? Of course there's no simple answer. But a peek at what's happened to the American family, the American neighborhood, and America itself helps us to understand why we sometimes long for days long gone:

The "typical" American family has become extinct. The *Monthly Labor Review* recently reported several dramatic changes in American families over the last 75 years. Among them:

- There has been a sharp rise in nonfamily households—consisting of people not related by blood, marriage, or adoption. From 1940 to 1989 the number multiplied tenfold—from 2.7 million nonfamily households to 27 million—with more than four fifths of these households occupied by a person living alone.
- For every two marriages, there is one divorce. Current patterns suggest that more than half of the marriages that took place during the '70s will end in divorce—double the ratio of the 1950s.

how come i feel so disconnected
if this is such a user-friendly world?

10

• Almost one fourth of family households with children are maintained by a single parent—nine out of ten are women.[2]

Nobody stays put. We've become a mobile society, traveling easily to new cities and building adventurous new lives. But along the way, we're scattering the landscape with bits and pieces of families once planted in one community over many generations. The owner of a local hardware store, whose father and grandfather knew when a neighbor was painting a room for the new baby or adding a portable closet for a visiting mother-in-law, today greets his anonymous customers as Sir and Ms.

No more block parties; it's the generation of backyard barbecues. Americans are on a privacy binge. No longer arriving anywhere unannounced, we congregate in fenced-in backyards rather than on front lawns and stoops. Days of making new friends at the laundromat are behind us; memories of having the time to meet for coffee are fading fast. Those who lived in tightly bound groups knew just where they belonged.

Today, we throw in our lonely loads of wash and fax our ideas back and forth. We chat by e-mail and order our holiday gifts through the Home Shopping Network. Enticing? Perhaps for some. But for most, "progress" has, by severely reducing human contact, left many of us feeling isolated and alone more often than we'd like.

Goodbye multipurpose relationships; now everything's specialized. Because our networks aren't clearly marked by neighborhood blocks and close-knit communities, we have to work harder to redefine them. Our relationships are separate and specialized, with different people to laugh with, confide in, borrow money from. These special people in our lives often don't know each other and may live miles apart—leaving us sometimes feeling fragmented rather than experiencing the sense of community we yearn for.

We carry our reputations in our wallets. If you ran short of cash at the supermarket, would the cashier let you write a personal check without first showing him a check-cashing card from the store? Would the local librarian allow you to borrow a book if you forgot your library card? If you went to a new doctor, would the secretary still smile if you told her you didn't have your checkbook but you'd send the payment as soon as possible?

> *"So in every individual the two trends, one toward personal happiness and the other toward unity with the rest of humanity, must contend with each other."*
>
> —*Sigmund Freud*

With so many strangers in our lives, we've developed an elaborate system of certification and surveillance. A wallet filled with ID cards vouches for who we are and that we can be trusted. When we're told that a doctor is licensed and certified, holds numerous degrees, and participates in a number of associations and organizations, we trust her without having yet met her. While it may be efficient, this system of validating our credentials leaves us feeling disconnected.

Ding dong, nobody's home. The facts don't lie: 56 million American women are in the workforce today, including 50 percent of women with children under one year of age.[3] The mass exodus of

how come i feel so disconnected
if this is such a user-friendly world?

12

Disconnection—When Do You Feel It Most?

Here are some of the recurring responses from those who admitted feeling a sense of alienation when we asked, "When do you feel lonely the most?"

- "When it's holiday time and my family is scattered all over the country—and we have to wish each other Happy New Year and send kisses over the phone."

- "When someone new moves into the neighborhood and I remember how I used to welcome every family with a cake and my friendship . . . and now I'm too rushed to get to the bakery and too tired to make small talk with strangers."

- "When I'm in the car. I feel like I'm in a space capsule— far removed from everyone."

- "When I'm shopping—in a megastore, where nobody smiles or even looks at me, where it takes me an hour to find what I'm looking for, and the store personnel could care less if I ever came back."

- "When I anxiously go to a new doctor's office and before the receptionist looks up to see my face, she hands me three pages of questions to answer and asks not why I'm there, but for my health insurance card to copy."

- "When it's dinner time and I'm preparing four different meals to be microwaved at different hours, because it's six o'clock and everyone in the family is at a different location."

women into the workplace has resulted in a nation of harried wives and mothers, stressed and tired husbands and fathers, latch-key children, and couples struggling to find time to breathe.

The Fuller Brush salesman, who used to be welcomed inside to chat and demonstrate his new products, now rings unanswered doorbells.

For stay-at-home moms, companionship is harder to find. For working moms, the stress of trying to squeeze into 24 hours what really needs 32 leads to the feeling of running on a perpetual treadmill. Men, too, are feeling the effects of disconnection—trying to keep up the pace and find some workable balance in their lives.

Heeere's TV. Television, mighty entertainer and teacher, companion, and babysitter, has made watching more appealing than playing and has created a passive generation of spectators. With 30-plus channels, there's something for everyone—Mom watches a four-hankie movie in the bedroom while Dad's in the den with Monday night football. The kids are scattered throughout the house tuned into *Murphy Brown,* MTV, and *The Simpsons.* A household of the '90s—with each family member unwinding in a different room. TV, originally intended to connect us with the world, has become a medium that fosters disconnection.

- IS ANYBODY HOME?

In researching this book we heard about a town in which each child, on entering kindergarten, is assigned to one family as a "storm child." If, while this child is in school, a sudden snow storm occurs, and if consequently the school buses cannot take the country children home in the afternoon, then the children are to go to their "storm homes" to be properly looked after.

One man shared that, as a little boy, he used to walk by this storm house every once in a while and try to imagine what it would be like when that great storm finally came. He would be all wet and cold. He would slowly climb the front porch steps and knock on the door

(text continued on page 17)

how come i feel so disconnected
if this is such a user-friendly world?

14

How Well Connected Are You?

Are you comfortably bonded, tethered, and tied to your world—or are feelings of isolation and loneliness frequent companions? Take our quiz and assess the strength of your connection.

PART I—Mark each of the following statements with *T* for *True* or *F* for *False*.

1. I wish my children knew my parents better.
2. I am satisfied with my level of connectedness.
3. Maintaining long-distance relationships is important to me.
4. I look forward to Thanksgiving and Christmas.
5. I tend to give too much credence to what people possess rather than who they are.
6. I tend to believe new is better than old, the complex more impressive than the simple.
7. I think of my family as more contracted than extended.
8. I have joined an interest club/community organization group in the last two years.
9. I am basically optimistic about the future.
10. It is important enough to me to supply my children with an extended family that I go out of my way to make it happen.
11. I find it easier to talk on the phone than to speak face-to-face.
12. My workplace is a home away from home.
13. I would change my job tomorrow if I could.
14. I know I can rely on my friends for encouragement and support.
15. I think loyalty is an old-fashioned and overrated concept in the '90s.
16. I have no idea who my great-grandparents were.
17. I look forward to the time when I can shop, bank, and rent videos from home.
18. This AA slogan reflects my feelings: "What other people think of me is none of my business."

19. I'd love to go to my high school reunion.

20. Companies like Ben & Jerry's and The Body Shop who do good public service deeds earn my respect.

SCORING:

Score 1 point each if you answered *True* to the following statements: 2, 3, 4, 8, 9, 10, 12, 14, 18, 19, 20.

Score 1 point each if you answered *False* to the following statements: 1, 5, 6, 7, 11, 13, 15, 16, 17.

If you scored 15–20: Good work! You're negotiating your way through our brave new world successfully, giving credit to your roots and respecting those on whom you lean.

If you scored 7–14: You're on the right track. You know what's missing. Now all you need is the energy and creativity to bring it home.

If you scored 0–6: Your life is harder than it has to be. Read through this book with an open mind. Good luck!

PART II—Circle the answer that best reflects how you feel.

1. Beepers and car phones are:

  a) two of the best inventions of the decade

  b) the curse of the '90s

  c) possessions that show you are more important than I am

2. When I'm on the phone I find I:

  a) lie more easily than in person

  b) can empty the dishwasher, fold the wash, and sign checks without skipping a beat

  c) cut conversations short because I hate the phone

3. When I disapprove of a friend's actions, most often I:

  a) ignore it—he didn't mean it

  b) confront him—if I don't tell him, who will?

  c) dump him—who needs this aggravation?

4. I think prenuptial agreements are:

  a) poison, trust-sapping contracts

  b) necessary protection for this day and age

  c) a sad symptom of the times

how come i feel so disconnected
if this is such a user-friendly world?

16

5. My neighbors are:

   a) invaluable when it comes to accepting UPS packages, feeding the cat when we're away, and disappearing the rest of the year

   b) nameless, faceless beings to me

   c) annoying

6. At one time or another I have heard my kids say to me:

   a) you don't even know who I am

   b) your taste sucks

   c) I can't believe you don't trust me!

7. Today a generation gap occurs when there's an age difference of:

   a) 20 years

   b) 10 years

   c) 6 years

8. If I ran into my clergyman, I'd feel:

   a) pleased to say hello

   b) embarrassed that I haven't seen him for six months

   c) stuck without anything to say

9. I find people who make eye contact to be:

   a) refreshing

   b) intimidating

   c) weird

10. My sense of community encompasses:

   a) my zip code

   b) my bedroom

   c) the world

11. After decades of loyalty, I've recently:

   a) changed political party affiliation

   b) rooted for a different football/basketball/baseball team

   c) become a fan of another late-night talk show host

12. The future:

   a) is scary

   b) looks bright

   c) will be doable

By now you've probably figured out that Part II is the test of your dreams—there are no wrong answers. Our hope is that it triggered a thought or two about your connecting habits.

and a nice old fat lady would answer and say, "You must be our storm child. I'm so glad to see you. Please come in and take off those wet boots and cold gloves and get yourself warm by our fire while I make you some hot chocolate." That's the way he'd imagined it for all the years he went to school.

His luck, all the snowstorms of his youth occurred either on the weekends or, if on a school day, between the hours of four in the afternoon and seven the next morning, so the need of a storm home never once arose. "Yet," he said, "for me as a child to know exactly where my storm home was located should I ever need it helped make me more secure, more trusting, more giving and charitable, because I knew that I could never really be threatened. Each child knew that if he had to go to his storm home, it would probably be pretty nice, and that the people who lived there would be glad to see him at long last."

This man's reminiscences remind us of how important it is, in an age of uncertain guideposts and disappearing landmarks, to provide for our children the same sense of security that the knowledge of this storm house gave to him.

Over the last decade, dozens of studies have corroborated the linear relationship between strong personal connections and good health—physical, mental, and spiritual. As the message is sinking in, many of us are reshaping our goals and our definition of success. We're seeking richer relationships with those around us in our families and our communities. We're striving to connect to large and noble purposes so that the spirit of giving and sharing may enrich our lives.

how come i feel so disconnected
if this is such a user-friendly world?

18

Connect!

"Connect!" was the message that Frank H. T. Rhodes, President of Cornell University, delivered to graduating students at their 1993 commencement. "For success in Life 101, first connect with things beyond your major, so that at the center of your life there is something strong and worthy. For four years plus you've focused your attention. That's good. But it's possible to be Phi Beta Kappa and still be a doughnut—empty at the core. Drink in the grandeur of existence. . . .

"Second, connect to some people—people whose poetry will illume your prose. . . .

"Third, I hope you will connect with some purpose, which I suspect will flow from your connections with people and things. . . . It is by using our skills and our knowledge in the service of ends that are worthwhile that they attain their true value. And it is by connecting things, people, and purpose in our lives that we discover ourselves!"

It isn't easy. But neither is childbirth, learning to use a computer, or losing ten pounds. Rarely do improvement and growth magically just happen. As you read this book, we urge you to keep in mind these premises that we hold to be true:

1. We need relationships, and relationships need time to cultivate themselves.

2. As hard as we may work at staying connected, there is no guarantee of success in all attempts.

3. The seriousness of not connecting outweighs the difficulty of making connections.

4. There is no one right way to stay connected. What pushes one person's buttons may not touch another. What works for one couple, family, friendship, or other relationship does not always click for another.

5. Staying connected must include commitment and should include enjoyment.

6. The process of staying connected is part of the product.

• Closing Thoughts

The Atlantic Monthly recently reported that there are approximately 600,000 living words in modern English and a few hundred thousand more in various stages of oblivion. But what interested us is this: Half of everything people say or read may be accounted for by only 43 words, and one fourth of all spoken and written English requires only nine words.

This is the kind of preposterous claim that many people find hard to believe, but the writer of the article proved it for himself. At random he selected an assortment of texts from around his house: everything from *Alice in Wonderland* to an automobile warranty, from the *Ritz Carlton Cookbook* to the Boy Scout Oath. He subjected these to a methodical and somewhat skeptical investigation, only to acknowledge that indeed, more than one fourth of all the texts consisted of nine little words.

Without prolonging the suspense, here they are, in alphabetical order: *and, be, have, it, of, the, to, will, you.* No bells and whistles—that's it.[4]

We can't help but be surprised at how unremarkable the words are. We tend to think of the important words as the big ones, the powerful nouns. But none of these words is a noun. In fact, each is powerless in itself. Each of the words needs other words to communicate. Each of the words is a helper, a connector. Without these words you can bring up a subject, but you cannot pursue it; you can start a conversation, but you cannot sustain it. Trendy words may come and go, but these, the least spectacular, least obvious,

> "A human life is like a single letter in the alphabet. It can be meaningless. Or it can be part of a great meaning."
> —National Planning Committee of Jewish Theological Seminary

how come i feel so disconnected
if this is such a user-friendly world?

20

least visible—these are the bedrock of our language. They bind thought to thought. They make speech possible.

As with our language, so with our lives. As much as we might think of ourselves as the powerful nouns, the subject of the sentence, and the title of the story, we cannot stand alone.

The nine words remind us of what our hearts already know: that we need each other; that our lives, like our words, thrive on connection; and that sometimes, what is least apparent is also what is most important.

chapter two

"Ask Not What Your Family Can Do for You . . ."

Championing Close Encounters of the Most Important Kind

*"We know it now, more than ever in this alienated and
hostile society, where the only real communication lies
in those primal acts of love and touch: man and
woman, mother and child, father and child,
human and human. What else endures?"*
—Marya Mannes

how come i feel so disconnected
if this is such a user-friendly world?

22

Lots of us spent the '80s straining to be our own best friend, compulsively looking out for number one and stretching to reach our full potential. Only recently have we begun to question whether all this self-centeredness was cost-effective. What many of us realized was that while we were looking in the mirror, the American family was at risk of becoming an endangered species. A healthy family begins with a strong partnership between husband and wife—a bond between spouses who are not only willing but anxious to invest time and energy in their marriage, practicing teamwork daily in order to build a strong foundation on which their future family can rest. To become models for our children, we have to "walk the walk" ourselves—illustrating the concept of family connections at their purest, most unselfish best. Unfortunately, we still have a ways to go.

- AND THEY LIVED HAPPILY
  EVER AFTER . . .

Why do some relationships cool and collapse while others endure for decades? Researchers are giving growing attention to this question, looking for the secrets of long-lasting love. Findings from a number of studies, supported by the personal theories of the couples below, have convinced us of the validity of these ten basic truths:

1. "We made a commitment to each other, and neither of us ever thought that giving up was an option. We knew that when things

got tough—which they did—we had the ability to work them out together."

Commitment, most would agree, is the number one ingredient in all successful, long-term relationships. Romantic love and the fantasy engendered by initial attraction yield to a more realistic and lasting relationship, grounded in everyday life.

2. "We have a lot in common."

"Opposites attract" may be true for magnets, but not for partners in a lasting relationship, says Frank Pittman, a psychiatrist in Atlanta and author of *Private Lies: Infidelity and the Betrayal of Intimacy*. Quite the contrary—it's a high level of "mutuality"—similar backgrounds, interests, customs, religions, IQs, and lifestyles—that's more vital for a couple's future happiness.[6]

Reality Check–Are We Intimate Enough?

The goal is intimacy: that emotional safety zone in which anger and anxiety dissipate. Although practitioners provide tips and advice galore, solid research on relationships is lacking. What we do know is this:

- A three-year study of almost 2,000 men and women ages 18 to 73 showed that fewer than 10 percent of the men fully disclose their feelings to their wives.[1]
- Men often avoid loving and open behavior because they want to retain power and mystery; they fear a show of feelings makes them weak.[2]
- In a 1990 *Time* magazine poll, 56 percent of women and 55 percent of men felt it's more difficult to have a good marriage today than it used to be.[3]
- Most couples spend less than 30 minutes a week sharing intimate thoughts.[4]
- Yet despite all that, 67 percent of the people polled in a *Family Circle* index rate their marriage as "excellent." And couples are more likely today than in 1971 (56 percent vs. 46 percent) to say their partner is sensitive to their needs.[5]

(text continues on page 25)

how come i feel so disconnected
if this is such a user-friendly world?

24

How Intimate Are You?

Read each question. Answer with *Never, Rarely, Often, or Always*.

1. I catch myself wanting to be right more than I want to work things out.
2. When I listen to my partner, my mind tends to wander.
3. I say "I love you" to my partner.
4. I praise my partner.
5. I identify with my partner's problems, hopes, and fears.
6. I exaggerate the importance of the "petty" stuff.
7. I have trouble letting go of a grudge.
8. I keep expecting life to be fair (50/50) and to get back exactly what I give.
9. I tend to compare my mate to whomever else is around.
10. I say "thank you" to my partner.
11. I am embarrassed when my partner tells a bad joke.
12. I feel good when my partner confides in me.
13. I'm afraid my partner won't understand if I share my private thoughts.
14. I know just what to do when my partner feels overwhelmed.
15. I feel close to my partner even when we're apart.
16. I am thin-skinned when criticized by my mate.
17. I have trouble letting my partner know when I am angry.
18. I can listen to my partner's problems without feeling that I have to come up with a solution.
19. I feel my partner doesn't mean it when he/she apologizes.
20. I am careful not to attack when I confront my partner.

SCORING:

For numbers 3, 4, 5, 10, 12, 14, 15, 18, 20: If you answered *Always* score 3 points; *Often* gets 2 points; *Rarely* deserves 1 point; and *Never* is a 0.

For numbers 1, 2, 6, 7, 8, 9, 11, 13, 16, 17, 19: Score yourself 3 points for each *Never;* 2 points for each *Rarely;* 1 point for *Often;* and 0 for every *Always*.

If you scored 0–15: It seems it's been a while since you've looked into your partner's eyes or listened carefully to his/her words. You have a ways to go to approach intimacy, but keep trying—getting there is as rewarding as arriving!

If you scored 16–45: Join the crowd. You've had a taste of how much better life could be as part of an intimate partnership, but circumstances, temperament, or just plain laziness prevent you from enjoying the comfort more connectedness can bring.

If you scored 46–60: Most of the world envies you! Your life partner is truly your best friend, and you don't take for granted the blessed state you've both created. You can take whatever the world dishes out because you can divide your woes . . . and conquer!

3. "We really like each other; we've always been best friends."

In a survey of 100 couples married 45 years or longer, researcher Sarah Kerr found that 81 percent said they laugh together one or more times each day. For these couples, being best friends and liking their spouse as a person were seen as the most important reasons their marriages lasted.[7]

4. "We listen to each other."

It's no secret that couples who discuss what's important to them are happier and more likely to endure. Communication is about learning not only how to express ourselves but how to listen as well. We may not always want to hear what our partner has to say, but it's vital to keeping those communication lines open.

5. "We still turn each other on."

how come i feel so disconnected
if this is such a user-friendly world?

26

Sex is important; daily kissing, flirting, and compliments imperative; and fidelity an absolute given. It may not be easy being spontaneous about sex, but adaptive couples learn how to make "play dates," and many say they get a thrill anticipating that tonight's the night.

6. "We share the power in our marriage."

Love respects equality. The lovers with the best chance for happiness are those who respect each other as equal partners and contribute equally to the relationship—without thoughts of one-upmanship.

7. "We've never gone to bed angry."

> *"I hope it has been clear that the dream of a marriage 'made in heaven' is totally unrealistic, and that every continuing man-woman relationship must be worked at, built, rebuilt, and continually refreshed by mutual personal growth."*
>
> —*Carl Rodgers*

Ninety-seven percent of the husbands and wives in Sarah Kerr's study rarely or never left the house after an argument. While the way they resolve arguments varies—some set a policy never to go to bed angry while others intentionally agree to sleep it off first; some deal with issues immediately while others let a problem rest until the right time arises to address it—the common thread is a commitment to resolution.[8]

8. "We don't always look for the fireworks."

The main ingredients in a loving relationship are passion and comfort, writes Michael S. Broder in *The Art of Staying Together*. Passion may be the spark that draws two people together, but it doesn't provide the stability to sustain a long-term relationship. A sharing of ease with each other is the day-to-day glue that bonds couples together.[9]

9. "We have realistic expectations of each other."

A quiz developed by Jeffry Larson, a marriage and family therapist at Brigham Young University, found a notable level of misconceptions and false expectations among the undergraduates who took the test. When students were asked to evaluate statements as True or False, more than 75 percent agreed that the more positive and negative information partners disclose, the greater their satisfaction. The truth, according to Larson, is that intimacy is enhanced only when these disclosures are mostly positive.[10]

Reality Check-The Changing Family

Did you know that:

- Today 16.6 million children—one in four—live with one parent: double the proportion of two decades ago.[11]
- The most popular days of the year for video rentals are the times when families traditionally focused on each other: New Year's, Thanksgiving, and Christmas week.[12]
- By the year 2000, 40 percent of all births will be out of wedlock. [13]
- The divorce rate is nine times higher than a century ago.[14]
- Sixty-three percent of 1,000 households polled by the *Los Angeles Times* felt that family life is less important to people today than when they were children.[15]
- Only 10 percent of the homes in America today are traditional breadwinner models—father going off to work and mother staying home to take care of the children.[16]
- Sixty-six percent of women ages 18 to 24 said that they would, if they had the opportunity, stay home and raise their children.[17]
- A Gallup poll reported that 81 percent of the respondents think it's harder to raise children today than it was a generation ago.[18]

10. "If we had it to do over again, we'd still choose each other."

The same corny jokes that were once embarrassing are now cute. The faux pas are awkwardly sweet, the imperfections endearing. For long-lasting couples still in love, it's called tolerance.

how come i feel so disconnected
if this is such a user-friendly world?

28

• And Then We Became Three

If championing a close encounter between spouses seems like enough of a challenge, adding children to the equation complicates the issue tenfold.

These are not particularly family-friendly times. No longer part of larger communities that supplied us with a sense of trust and well being, we are on our own to furnish our families with a sense of loyalty, stability, and moral presence.

Statistics on the ways families have changed are troubling. Nothing is worth sacrificing the sense of belonging that keeps us together and keeps us whole, that enables us to transcend the outside forces that are capable of pulling us apart. Having a heritage to live up to, sharing common memories and goals, knowing there are people whose unconditional support we can always count on—these goals should be our bottom line. The welfare of the whole family is far more important than the good life of any individual member.

Build family loyalty. It is up to the family unit to reinforce the value of loyalty.

When the sailing's smooth, it's easy to stand by the members of our family. When the going gets tough, it's harder to be loyal to our loved ones, who suddenly may not seem so loving. Those moments when jumping ship seems like the preferred alternative are the most critical times to hang on.

According to Dr. Michael Peltzman, a Long Island, New York, psychologist specializing in families, if family loyalty is built and reinforced during good times, those bonds will help overcome temporary setbacks.

How to build family loyalty? There are no hard and fast rules, says Dr. Peltzman. But here are a few guidelines:

• Show your family in both word and action how much you love and appreciate them. A daily unsolicited favor or gesture of kindness, taking the time to say "I love you," "You are important to me," or "Thank you for doing that for me," covers a lot of ground.

• Find ways to do things with and for the family as a whole. Don't be afraid of mandating certain appearances by family law. If the priorities are understood, the resistance will be less.

• Reinforce the importance of keeping details of your intimate family life away from outsiders. Never complain to outsiders about family members.

> *"The dark, uneasy world of family life—where the greatest can fail and the humblest succeed."*
> *—Randall Jarrell*

• Don't demand or expect perfection. Give family members space to feel free to experiment, take risks, change patterns of behavior, and dare to make mistakes without fear of ridicule or rejection. Help each other grow.

• Reinforce to each other that your family is extraordinary and separate from the rest of the world. There is a sort of "covenant" that binds spouses to each other, parents to children, and children to parents, that has to be the bedrock of what's expressed by the overused phrase "family values."

We have to acknowledge that our kids learn their behavior by observing ours—not by just listening to our words. If we want our chil-

how come i feel so disconnected
if this is such a user-friendly world?

30

> *"Children have never been very good at listening to their elders, but they have never failed to imitate them."*
>
> —*James Baldwin*

dren to demonstrate commitment and caring now and later in life, we have to practice these qualities ourselves . . . daily. When we give our kids more experiences than things, when we do our best to instill a sense of purpose and the ability to make a difference, we assure that the future world our children will live in will be a richer one.

View each person in the family as a crucial, interdependent member of the team.

Build unity by making sure each family member is aware of how important he or she is. Being breadwinners, chauffeurs, cooks, housekeepers, and disciplinarians sometimes overshadows parents' most important role: unconditional supporter and self-esteem reinforcer.

People feel most connected to each other when our input is valued and our contributions appreciated. These bonds are solidified when we help each other. Parents help most not when they "do for," but when they make themselves dispensable. Just like on any team, different people should play different positions according to their ability to get the job done. The pace of life in the '90s demands a "we're all in this together" attitude. We have to convince our families that the rewards of teamwork are well worth the effort. Here are some approaches you might find successful.

With your spouse:

1. The rational approach. "If both of us work together this afternoon to get the house in order, instead of you watching TV and me growling at you as I vacuum under your feet, we'll have tonight to have some fun, with neither of us feeling tired or resentful."

2. The good health approach. Marriage and family therapist John Gottman studied 73 couples over a four-year period and found that men who did housework were far healthier than those who did not. Helpful men were not as overwhelmed by their wives' emotions and had lower heart rates during marital conflict than men who did no housework.[19]

3. The "it's the '90s" approach. Respecting your wife as an equal; valuing the integrity of her career as you do your own; and being reliable, independent, and a true partner is today's definition of masculine. Ignorance is . . . ignorance. Today's wimp is not the guy cleaning the fish tank but the one who can't find the ketchup. "Macho" has gone the way of the Bee Gees, junk bonds, and rotary phones.

4. The "I promise I won't look too closely" approach. Acknowledge that each partner may have a different timetable and a different definition of clean. Compromising on what tasks are the most palatable and when a given chore has to be completed (maybe a week to do a list posted on the refrigerator?) is crucial. Agree not to remind or prod in between and accept the results without criticizing. So what if you can do it faster and better—if you have to do it alone?

5. The "I will appeal to your sense of justice" approach. A black-and-white accounting of the time each partner spends on

how come i feel so disconnected
if this is such a user-friendly world?

32

housework has to wake up the most complacent partner. A more equitable settlement can be reached by assessing how balanced your situation is, renegotiating changes, and dividing tasks according to the amount of time each partner spends at home.

6. The "boost to intimacy" approach. The development of new domestic skills will be rewarded with a sense of accomplishment and pleasure. Closeness comes from sharing, and men who feel like strangers in their own homes ("Where is the Ajax?"—or worse—"What is Ajax?"), who regard helping with housework as a loss to their standard of living, must hold themselves accountable for a resentment that can prevent true intimacy from occurring.

And with the kids:

7. Adapt the approaches above. Try #1 ("Let's work together and then go to the amusement park"), #4 ("I promise I won't yell if you overcook the spaghetti or miss the corners when you vacuum"), #5 ("You're old enough to understand that Mom can't do it all" or "I don't care if you're a boy or a girl—you are capable of cleaning this brownie pan and cleaning up the dog's mess!")

Use family consultations to settle the tugs-of-war that pull on your family.

Conflicts inevitably arise within families.

• A family vacation: Dad wants to play golf; Mom wants the beach; Jamie wants to ski; Donny wants to stay home with his friends.

• Julie's curfew: Mom says midnight; Julie says, "No fair! All my friends can stay out till 1 a.m."; Dad looks from one to the other and shrugs.

• A house to be cleaned: "I'm no good at making beds!" "I hate taking out the garbage!" "Who will set the table, empty the dishwasher?"

Family consultations are a technique that might make the struggle a bit less stressful. For a team effort in problem solving, follow these five steps:

1. Clarify the issue— what needs to be decided, planned, or resolved? For example: Now that Mom has gone back to work, she's overloaded with family chores and needs cooperation for a more efficient division of labor.

A Family Intimacy Workout

On a given weekday night—aided and abetted by some popcorn, an unplugged phone, and every family member's undivided attention—put as many of these questions in a hat as you have family members. Let each one pull out a slip and answer the question.

• What do you remember as the happiest moment we ever shared together?
• Go around the room and name the quality you admire most in each person.
• Without embarrassing the person, tell the funniest time you shared with somebody in the family.
• Describe your favorite Christmas or holiday.
• What's the first memory you can recall?
• Tell about a situation you handled masterfully this past month, and credit a family member for helping you be successful.
• Tell each person the present you'd love to buy him/her if you had the money.
• Go around the room and tell the three things you'd miss most about that person if he/she went away for a year.
• If you were casting a movie about your family, who would you have play each family member's part?
• Share the most recent considerate gesture a family member made for you that went unmentioned.

how come i feel so disconnected
if this is such a user-friendly world?

34

Mantras to Help Stay on Track During Family Consultations

Having the right attitude is most important in family consultations. If you're willing to commit to the concept, repeat these mantras to help keep you on track:

1. I will listen to every suggestion with respect and an open mind—no matter how silly it might sound.

2. I won't interrupt. (Families might borrow a custom from the Tlingit Tribe of southeastern Alaska. To prevent interruptions during a consultation, they use a beautifully carved "talking stick," held by the person speaking. As long as that person holds the stick, no one else may speak.)

3. I will not think in terms of "What's in it for me?" but instead, "What's good for all of us?"

4. I will be patient and remember that solutions don't always come quickly and easily.

5. I will be creative and willing to inject some humor into the sessions. The more ideas we all contribute, the better our chance of finding one that will win family approval.

2. Explore all the facts relating to the situation. Try answering: Who? What? Where? When? Why? and How? Who could walk the dog? What are reasonable responsibilities for a 10-year-old? When can jobs be rotated? How can you assign the jobs that nobody wants?

3. Brainstorm. Bring out different ideas for plans or solutions. "What if we spin a wheel to assign the jobs?" "How about a monthly rotation?" "Can we trade jobs?" "Maybe the little kids can be included in jobs like watering the plants and folding towels." "I'll do all the laundry if I never have to clean a bathroom!"

4. Decide as a group on the best decision. Make sure that nobody feels unduly burdened. "The vote on the plan was unanimous—

Mom will make the chart and we'll spin for the month of March; then we'll meet again for a family pow-wow in two weeks to see how it's working. If everything is OK, we'll rotate in April."

5. Carry out this decision with a spirit of unity. The benefits include the reappearance of Mom's specialty lasagna dish, as well as the satisfaction of feeling like an integral part of the team.[20]

Simple enough? Not at first, but practice brings improvement. Begin with not-so-important and not-so-serious decisions (What movie should we see? What should we buy Grandma for her birthday?) just to get the hang of the process.

Subjects that qualify for consultation are those that concern part or all of the family and that benefit from the input of everyone's ideas. Issues of health, safety, and morality are automatically exempt. Consultations should include laughter and fun so that everyone will look forward to the next one.

Be comfortable in your role as an authority. Your children have enough friends.

Many parents who are "yes-ers" tend to abdicate their role in making their children more responsible for a goal they see as immediately more satisfying—making their children happy. Every time we unwillingly give in, reluctantly stretch the rules, or allow ourselves to be cowed by the mythic "everyone else's parents," we deny our children the comfort that comes with secure boundaries. Saying "yes" when we'd much rather say "no" is following a policy of appeasement that just about assures that there'll be trouble ahead.

how come i feel so disconnected
if this is such a user-friendly world?

36

Of course, before you say "no," you will have carefully listened to your children's arguments, without judgment or criticism. Often that means swallowing what you don't like hearing. If you're critical of what's shared with you, the message your kids will get is, "It's easier if I keep my mouth shut." When children know you're listening with respect and want to understand their feelings, they'll be more eager to share their thoughts and experiences. While listening, keep these *don'ts* in mind: don't interrupt; don't contradict; don't lecture; and don't interrogate.

Our goal should be to find ways to help our children become humane and strong. In times of disagreement, when the going gets rough, we have to remember that it's by focusing on solutions and lending a helping hand—not by assigning blame—that we raise children who respect each other and are sensitive to the needs and feelings of others.

Don't forget:

- Listen first—then offer your opinion.
- Don't back off. Stick to your guns. Regardless of what they think, kids are not ready to run their lives without your supervision.
- Take your kids seriously—no matter how way out and weird their point may be.
- Let your kids make decisions appropriate to their age and level of maturity . . . after they understand from your actions and words what you expect.
- Be flexible. Rules are necessary, but bending is allowed.

• After a blow-up, forgive, forget, and keep on trusting. Remember: your love is unconditional.

• Develop a relationship with your children's friends. Be welcoming in your home.

• Invest the time. It always pays.

Use the dinner hour as a time for family connections. Dinner is an opportunity to refuel, relax, and relate.

A 1990 *New York Times* poll revealed that 74 percent of the 555 adults surveyed rated eating dinner together with their family a priority of utmost importance. Research shows that eating dinner as a family contributes to building self-esteem in our children and helps families survive tough times. Why then, if we know it's one of the best things we can do to cement family bonds, is it so difficult to find 30 minutes of uninterrupted togetherness?[21]

In November 1993, Oprah Winfrey interviewed five families who volunteered to participate in an experiment. They agreed to eat dinner together for an uninterrupted half hour, at least four times each week for a month. What seemed at first to be no big deal proved a greater challenge than any of them anticipated. "It didn't feel normal," confessed one member of a participating family. Others said, "Our schedules were so hectic, we sometimes had to eat at nine to keep to the deal"; "We could only sit still for 10–15 minutes; we flunked the test"; and "The hardest part of the experiment was living without a daily dose of 'Star Trek.'"

how come i feel so disconnected
if this is such a user-friendly world?

38

"Mommy, Can I Go to Work with You?"

"My daughter asked many times if she could come with me to work but I never took her requests seriously," says Holly, a newspaper reporter. "A newspaper office is hectic and rushed, often bordering on frantic—not the kind of atmosphere where I thought she'd enjoy spending a day. I finally agreed to be politically correct on National Take-Your-Daughter-to-Work Day. I was on deadline, covering a story on homeless shelters, and didn't know how much attention I could give her.

"But she was a trouper. While I was intense at my computer, she was content to watch my coworkers with more easily observable jobs—in layout, graphics, advertising, and sales. At lunch I showed her around but was still wondering what was going on inside that 9-year-old mind . . . until I heard her on the phone that night with her best friend, emphatically stating that when she grows up she wants to be a reporter just like her mom."

One Illinois family, whose mom had to travel for business to New York during the month of the experiment, ate dinner together with the help of conference calls. From her hotel room, Mom ate dinner on her bed and conversed with her family over the phone for the required half hour. In Illinois, at Mom's place at the table sat the telephone. Her voice could be heard by her husband and children, chatting away about her day and asking all about theirs. So, Oprah, were they cheating—or being creative? Keep in mind that:

• Mealtimes should be occasions for peaceful nourishment—for moments in which family members can interact in a comfortable and intimate environment.

• Family connections hinge on conversation. We should use the dinner table as a place to feel safe and to share thoughts, incidents, and anecdotes. If conversation doesn't flow spontaneously, help it along by choosing a topic from the news or a current issue of controversy. Or more personally, ask triggering questions like, "Did any of your teachers do anything silly today?" "If you could change one thing that happened today, what would it be?"

• The dinner table is a place for praise and positive messages— not a battleground where we punish, criticize, interrogate, or confront. Leave those unpleasantries for later.

• Turn on the answering machine and turn off the TV; put away the newspaper and video games; and mandate dinner as an interruption-free zone.

• Don't expect every family mealtime to be a great success. But don't give up. Remember that sharing meals builds family identity and solidarity.

Make time to spend with your kids. Togetherness doesn't just happen—in today's world it has to be planned.

Can you remember the last time you:

• Played hooky and did something frivolous with one or more of your children?

• Took a family car ride and enjoyed the time to sing and play word games—without Nintendo or a Walkman in sight?

• Watched a TV show as a family—on one TV, in one room?

• Took one or more of your kids to work?

• Had a tea party with one of your children—just to catch up on life?

how come i feel so disconnected
if this is such a user-friendly world?

40

- Acknowledged an accomplishment (an outstanding report card, a five-pound weight loss, a job promotion, most-improved award from the soccer coach) with a family celebration?
- Played a board game—from start to finish?
- Had an uninterrupted dinner together four times in one week?

If you answered "today," "yesterday," or "this week" more than three times—bravo! You do indeed make time to stay connected with your family. If not, take comfort in the fact that you're far from alone. Close families don't just happen—staying close requires constant effort. We can't connect and remain static; as families, we are not finished products, but part of a healthy process in which we all continuously grow and change.

Be creative with vacation options. Traveling with your kids doesn't mean sacrificing your vacation.

Years ago, a family vacation might have meant getting into the car and driving fifty miles to visit grandma and grandpa or traveling to the family bungalow, where aunts, uncles, and cousins converged for a weekend, week, or fortnight together.

The world is a lot different today, and so are most vacations. Affordable airfares, superhighways, charge cards, and families with many varied interests and tastes have broadened our concept of how to travel successfully married . . . with children.

According to a study conducted by RY&P/Yankelovich Partners, 43 percent of American adults took a pleasure trip with children in 1993. And one out of four adults identified children's programs as crucial in planning a trip.[22] With that in mind, the travel industry—from hotel chains to packaged tours and cruise lines—are responding with special features and programs to please all ages. Today a family vacation can be a restful getaway or a wild adventure, near home or in exotic climates—pleasing both adults and kids.

It's time to expand your definition of a family vacation beyond Disney World. How about giving one of these a try?

"All that in one hotel?" Some of the nation's large hotel chains have introduced camps and children's clubs to keep kids busy while their moms and dads do their thing. From pizza parties to kite-flying contests—child-oriented activities and events are plentiful and there's no such word as boredom.

"I'm joining this club forever!" Bless the one-fee-pays-all policy! Originally designed for singles, these get-away-from-it-all hot spots have expanded to offer an assortment of activities for kids and their parents to enjoy—separately or together. Club Med, the recognized leader in the field with more than 100 vacation villages worldwide; Club Getaway in the Berkshire Mountains; and several clubs in Jamaica are among the resorts that offer sparkling beaches, breathtaking sunsets, and nonstop activities day and night.

"Hey, mate!" The same "club" concept has been adapted to cruises. There are supervised camp activities and babysitting services, playrooms, wading pools, video arcades, and discos.

how come i feel so disconnected
if this is such a user-friendly world?

42

"Let's travel backwards in time. . . ." Some towns are especially famous for reflecting a specific period in history. How about Old Sturbridge Village in Sturbridge, Massachusetts—a New England town of the 1830s. Or colonial Williamsburg, in Virginia—a living recreation of colonial life 250 years ago. From the French Quarter in New Orleans to Amish Country in Lancaster, Pennsylvania, share the experience of reliving history along with sunburn, rides, and quality time.

"Climb, row, paddle . . . my muscles are killing me!" What could be better to promote family bonding than paddling together for five hours down the rapids of the Delaware River on a four-person raft? Or hiking and climbing the red rocks of Arizona? Families who enjoy physically exertive vacations will share, along with togetherness, the thrill of adventure and the challenge of testing their strength and their endurance.

A Family That Skis Together

"It was never my idea to take up skiing," admits George, a high school principal. *"But when my kids decided they wanted to learn to ski, it was either learn with them or be left home alone. During our first winter of group lessons we had many laughs—mostly at my expense. Eventually we got the hang of the sport and became a family of ski fanatics.*

"Our days of vacations on the beach are history; now every school holiday we head for the mountains. With the kids in college it's harder to synchronize our schedules, but somehow, when snow beckons, we follow!

"Last month, when my older son won a raffle from a local sports store—a four-day ski trip for two to Aspen, all expenses paid—he invited me to be his partner. After hearing him say there was no one he'd rather spend the four days with, I knew that the decision to learn to ski had been one of my best!"

"It's mind over matter. . . . " A religious retreat is a vacation enjoyed by a growing number of families—a message that many of us are searching for peace of mind. At retreats, seminars are offered on ethical and social issues—after which families pursue quiet activities like yoga and meditation—with opportunities provided to practice restoring mental balance.

Be a cool parent . . . but not too cool. It's easy to push the wrong buttons with our kids.

Among the parents we surveyed, when we asked, "How do you most easily turn your kids off?"—this is what we heard:

1. "When I lecture."

Boo, hiss to any sentence beginning with, "When I was your age . . ." or "Now just listen . . ." What good is our lesson if our kids tune out? Sometimes our words are better received if sent indirectly. ("Did you read the article about the kid who was driving drunk—and now he's paralyzed?" "Did you hear about the girl who had a party for the entire eleventh grade while her parents were away, and one of the kids accidentally started a fire?") If we can be convincing without lecturing, our kids will be more open to listening.

2. "When I use cliches."

Some of the worst, recycled through the decades, are:

- "When you have children of your own, you'll understand."
- "This is for your own good."
- "Some day you'll thank me for this."

how come i feel so disconnected
if this is such a user-friendly world?

44

First We'll Laugh . . . Then Let's Talk

"We were driving our son's car when we heard a rattle coming from the trunk," recalls Norm, a high school teacher and father of an 18-year-old. *"So we pulled over, opened the trunk, and saw 3 six-packs of beer, clinking away. We were definitely angry, but not sure how to deal with our son. Then our plan evolved . . . When we got home we gathered our props, and, from the driveway, called upstairs, 'Adam, won't you join us? The bar's open.' His mouth dropped open.*

"A good laugh allowed us to ease into a serious discussion about responsibility and the drinking age—without an attitude problem from our son. I think we kept the door open and showed him that even though we're not about to look the other way, we can deal with this situation firmly without sacrificing a sense of humor."

- "You don't know easy you've got it."
- "Believe me, this hurts me more than it hurts you."

3. "When I compare my kids unfavorably to others."

Avoid questions like "Why can't you keep your room clean like your brother does?" or "Amanda's mom told me she got a 96 on the chemistry midterm; what happened to you?" While meant to motivate, they are a definite turn-off.

4. "When I generalize."

When we say, "You never think about anyone else's feelings" or "You're always so careless," our kids hear, "You're a disappointment; you're hopeless." These statements are deadly for kids' self-esteem and totally ineffective in getting them to change. Global attacks that begin with "You . . ." followed by a negative ("You're spoiled, lazy, a slob, etc.") put kids on the defensive and reduce whatever chances we might have had for getting a reasonable response.

5. "When I threaten—especially when my threats are idle, irrational, or impossible to carry out."

Most often when we threaten ("I've had it with you; if you're one minute late for curfew, you're grounded for a month" or "If you leave your clothes all over the floor, I won't buy you another thing this year!") we've lost control of a situation. Our kids' reaction may range from not taking us seriously to testing us by repeating the offense—just to see what we'll do.

6. "When I speak without thinking first."

Like: "Late again? What else could I expect from you lately?" instead of "I'm upset that you're an hour late; I was worried that something terrible happened." Or "You're dressed totally inappropriately" instead of "Do you think you might take out the nose ring for your job interview?" Trying to stay close often means quelling our frustration and coming up with softer, more subtle words. Instead of "Why are you in a bad mood? Everyone should have as good a life as you do!"—how about "You're in a bad mood for no reason? Come here and let me give you a hug."

7. "When I try to be too much of a pal."

We may dress and act like we're 17 and try to use teen language ("I can't believe you dissed me!")—thinking that we're bonding. But what we're really doing is embarrassing ourselves. Kids, especially teenagers, don't want parents for pals; peers are much more satisfying. Of course they want us to be understanding, lenient, and fun—but appropriately so in our role as their parents.

And from the same parents . . . In response to "So how do you bridge the generation gap with your kids?"—the consensus was:

how come i feel so disconnected
if this is such a user-friendly world?

46

Would You Translate That, Please?

The generation gap between parents and their teenage offspring can make communication, let alone connecting, a trying ordeal.

What teens say is almost never what they mean. Take, for example, this statement: "Amy's mom said it's OK with her." What that really means is, "Amy didn't ask her mother yet, but if you say OK, then we'll get her mother to agree too."

- "It's not so cold out." Translation: "I don't like my winter coat" or "I left my coat in school."
- "There's not so much snow." Translation: "Do you really expect me to wear those nerdy boots?"
- "I don't have any homework." Translation: "I forgot my book in school."
- "I don't know when it's due." Translation: "It's due tomorrow."
- "Can you help me with this?" Translation: "It was due today."

Then there's language reserved for moments of confrontation.

- "I'll take care of it" means "Here's the deal—I'll act like I'm taking this seriously and you act like you believe me."
- "That's not how we do things now" and "You don't understand" are tactical expressions designed to convey that you're too old to know what's going on.[23]

- Remain open to discussion, negotiation, and compromise. "If you insist on ripped jeans, that's OK, but I'm not going to pay for them." "Wear whatever you want to school, but in church you must dress appropriately."
- Work at being consistent. Don't let a disrespectful quip slide three times, then suddenly explode on the fourth. Be clear as to what you expect from them and what they can expect from you—and then follow through.
- Call for a "time out" when issues become too heated.

Realize that when emotions are heated, cool rational thought is half an hour away.

- Recognize that fads and behaviors are temporary. Get through the tough ones by chanting, "This too shall pass . . ."
- Don't allow yourself to forget that you were once a kid too.

- CLOSING THOUGHTS

There is a quote attributed to Billy Martin: "Baseball is losing. We lost 62 games but we won 100 and got the pennant." The message—that even with a lot of trying, some degree of failure is inevitable—is a perfect one to remember when we fall short of doing the right thing, saying the right thing, or gracefully rising to the occasion within the arena of our families.

If today we feel responsible for an error that cost our team the big game (or a disastrous dinner hour), tomorrow offers the opportunity to incorporate what we learned from our mistakes to assure a more positive encounter. Families can be harsh in their criticism, but it's in the nature of most to be flexible and forgiving.

Look to your immediate family. If you don't feel satisfied by the intimacy and closeness you observe, maybe you've just been on cruise control too long. A great Hassidic rabbi once said that if you are going east and you suddenly decide you want to go west, all you need is the awareness that you have the strength to turn yourself around. We can gain that awareness from our errors and impart it to the most important others in our lives.

chapter three

"I Feel Certifiable . . . It Must Be Thanksgiving"

Making Friends with Your Family and Other Strangers

"No him, no me."
—Dizzy Gillespie on Louis Armstrong

how come i feel so disconnected
if this is such a user-friendly world?

50

The social and economic direction of our whole culture places the family at the center of our lives. The fantasy of living without secrets in an atmosphere of acceptance and trust, where love is unconditional and support is a birthright, is the '90s impossible dream. Families name us, root us, and supply a touchstone to which each member can return to be recharged and renewed. They also define us with their unique package of rivalries, tensions, jealousies, and angers. Like magnets, they alternately tempt us to bond closer and then repel, leaving us scrambling to extricate ourselves from their influence.

The family's tug on the fabric of our lives is undeniably powerful. And the task of recreating (or creating for the first time) a refuge of comfort and peace, complete with everything good that families mean to the children who are part of them, is one of the hardest challenges of our lives.

Close extended families might be rarer than they once were, but they're far from outmoded or irrelevant. In fact, to be part of such a family is probably one of the few things in the world that are universally envied. Although young people in their 20s are not rushing out to create their branch of the family tree—they're getting married in fewer numbers, marrying later, and having fewer children—they still yearn for the comfort supplied by those with whom they share ancestors and last names.

The strength of family ties can withstand separations and long distances. But when families are face to face, the fun begins! We might enjoy our friends more, but it's our relatives to whom we turn in times of crisis. Parents and adult children are each other's preeminent sources of both financial aid and care when illness and infirmity strike.

Reality Check–Dysfunctional? Not Us!

We hear a lot of sighing about "what was," but the facts show that:

- One in two adult children chooses to live within 25 miles of parents, and one in four lives within five miles.[1]
- Forty-one percent of women and 45 percent of men think multigenerational households are a good idea.[2]
- Sixty-three percent of those responding to the National Survey of Family and Households claimed a sibling as a best friend.[3]

Our siblings are almost as supportive, with the added bonus of being practically as sociable as our friends.

The life expectancy of the relationships between members of our densely connected extended families is forever. With that in mind, we look to our holidays and celebrations for the elusive, soul-satisfying bonding we know exists somewhere in this world.

Columnist Ellen Goodman says that "holidays have become our performance art. The holidays become overloaded with what's missing the rest of the year. A take-out generation springs for a whole turkey and never mind the leftovers. A scattered family pushes home through airports and highways to sit on folding chairs. A great deal is riding on the performance. And the reviews."[4]

With a touch more empathy and a tad more flexibility, the promise can be fulfilled.

how come i feel so disconnected
if this is such a user-friendly world?

52

Those Were the Days . . .

"When I grew up in Brooklyn," says Jill, a mother of three, "my family's commitment to each other came first—before friendships, before work, and certainly before individual satisfaction. There was a cousin's club, which rotated locations every six weeks on Sundays. Three generations, ten different families, got together to eat, argue, laugh, and bond. In the summers we split up into three different bungalow colonies.

"There were over 400 such communities in those days, in the Catskill Mountains. The mothers played mahjong, the fathers who came up on the weekends played pinochle and smoked cigars, and the kids grew up as safe and protected as humanly possible. We returned year after year like swallows to Capistrano.

"Today my parents live in Florida. My kids never really had the chance to know them, let alone my aunts, uncles, and cousins. Today their image of grandma is a woman who travels, works out in a health spa, dyes her hair, buys generous birthday presents, and is very proud of them . . . through their accomplishments."

It doesn't make a difference who Mom liked better. Get over it, and turn your sister or brother into your friend.

Our society has words for parenting—mothering and fathering—but none to describe the relationship between brothers and sisters, those we grew up with, sharing blood and history on a most intimate and profound level. That spooky knowledge of someone who is utterly like and unlike us shapes the image of who we are and who we dare to become.

With the awesome ability to read someone so well comes the knowledge of how to strike their sensitive nerves most effectively. Because one third of adult siblings describe their childhood relationships as "competitive," "humiliating," and "hurtful," it is no surprise that millions more brothers and sisters love each other than like each other.[5]

Whether the bond we share with our siblings is one of our most successful or one of our most debilitating depends on how important stability in our relationship is to us. When expectations for closeness are disappointed, the hurt can be deep and lifelong. But there's always room for growth, renewal, and repair.

We may not be able to rewrite history, but we can try to find new ways to forgive and forget, tightening one of our oldest connections along the way.

Reality Check–Did You Know That:

- Ties with siblings are stronger for adults with better education and better incomes.[6]
- Women are more likely to keep up ties with their siblings than men are. Ties between sisters are likely to be the closest, ties between brothers the most rivalry-filled and competitive.[7]
- Siblings are most important to the family support network of younger adults. As adults have their own children, and then adult children, to rely on, contact with brothers and sisters diminishes.[8]
- While older adults have less contact with siblings, they feel they can call on them for support. Rivalries forged in earlier years become less important, allowing siblings to play an increasingly strong role in sustaining a feeling of embeddedness and integration in old age.[9]

Prepare in advance. If holiday get-togethers at your parents' house are usually disasters, try a restaurant instead. A new environment makes it easier to avoid repeating old patterns.

Understand the problem. If we can make sense of where the difficulties originated—whether it's past favoritism or one sibling resembling a parent another had difficulty with—we've taken the first step toward lessening the rivalry. Talk to a therapist, a spouse, a friend . . . and then of course your sibling.

how come i feel so disconnected
if this is such a user-friendly world?

54

Make time alone a priority. Two thirds of siblings in a study of adult siblings said that the marriages of their brothers and sisters drove a wedge between them.[10] If that's the case, make time to see your sibling alone.

Use your kids. For those who've carried childhood rivalry into adulthood, the next generation can be the catalyst to revitalize a family connection. According to Michael Kahn, Ph.D., coauthor of *The Sibling Bond* and professor of clinical psychology at the University of Hartford, having kids can forge a bond that never existed before, if siblings unite in creating new roles for themselves as parents. Even if siblings are too wary to say "I love you" directly, they can do it through each other's children.[11]

Focus on your unique past. Who else but a sibling can remember the smells of Grandma's kitchen, the way Uncle George followed fire engines no matter where he was originally headed, the way Aunt Sophie always guessed what time it was because she was too vain to put on her glasses . . . ?

In a more perfect world, adult siblings would cherish childhood memories and, through these

Long-Distance Sisters

"My sister doesn't get me," admits Jackie, now 38 years old. "She buys the most inappropriate birthday presents, never understands my sarcasm, and thinks I'm too much of a pushover in raising my kids. Yet, when we're on the phone, our voices eerily reflect the same nuances. We both overuse Brillo for most of the chores we use it for, and we both cover our eyes at exactly the same moment in the movies. We can't lie to each other, and most times we can't tell the truth either. It's easier not to be around each other too often."

memories, find understanding and enrichment. They would rely on each other and be part of each other's support network. Because this is a less-than-perfect world, we sometimes have to remind ourselves that relationships have to be worked on and maintained to stay in tip-top running order. Stay focused on your shared positive past . . . and a more perfect shared present will follow.

Visualize what it feels like to walk in your parents' shoes. Both generations will benefit from the empathy.

To strengthen our most basic bond, the parent-child relationship has to move more toward a respectful, adult-adult relationship. Both sides must refuse to get hooked into a repetition of old charges and countercharges. They have to loosen up, be flexible, and be willing to negotiate change.

When the relationship is healthy, each allows the other to retain a strong sense of self while willingly giving up some of his or her power to enrich the relationship. Each has the ability to wound with a few words and dampen each other's mood with a glance. Each can frustrate, misunderstand, and disappoint without really trying. And both have memories of too many moments marked by friction, coldness, and withdrawal.

As children, we must stop giving double messages—one time asking for advice and financial aid, the next time screaming for parents to quit meddling. Problems occur because it's as natural for us to want to live our own lives, work out our own destinies, even

how come i feel so disconnected
if this is such a user-friendly world?

56

make our own mistakes, as it is for our parents to stay within their stereotypical controlling and worrying mode.

· I F   O N L Y   T H E Y   W O U L D . . .

We asked the couples we interviewed for their wish list of behaviors they'd like to see their parents change. Their answers came out fast and furiously. It was clear they saw themselves as wronged—constantly provoked by unchanging parental expectations. To the unfinished statement, "I wish my parents would . . . ," they said:

· "Offer support instead of a lecture if I describe how I'm going through a tough time."

· "Stop being so judgmental about how I spend my money and how I discipline my children."

· "Accept me as my own person, not just a reflection or extension of them."

· "Initiate calls and visits more themselves rather than always expecting me to do it."

· "Give advice when it's asked for—not all the time."

· "Respect my opinions, including and especially the ones that differ from theirs."

· "Show more interest in what I'm doing rather than just expect me to care about what's happening in their lives."

· "Forget about ancient transgressions and rebellions and realize I'm not a teenager anymore."

· "Cease and desist from making me feel guilty . . . for breathing."

Then we asked parents of adult children the same question. It was interesting to see how many of these issues were the same. When asked to complete, "I wish my children would . . . ," they responded with:

- "Not misunderstand our interest as an invasion of their privacy."
- "Be more appreciative of what we've done for them."
- "Let go of the anger they feel for mistakes we made in raising them."
- "Be more respectful."
- "Visit more often."
- "Show more of an interest in what we do with our lives."
- "Stop bad-mouthing their brothers and sisters to us."
- "Just listen and not get so defensive if we make a suggestion."

Language to Connect Us

Nothing energizes us into our fight-flight posture as quickly as our parents' old standby expressions. Most of the time, "Call me the minute you get home," "We don't want to impose," or "Take home this care package," while meant as loving gestures, can be irritating when unasked for or unwanted. We've got to remember that it's as difficult for our parents to stop seeing us in need of rescuing as it is for us to stop wanting their approval.

Among families we interviewed, the following suggestions resulted in successful bonding experiences.

- An unexpected call, card, or gift . . . especially a clipping or cartoon with a note, "This made me think of you."
- Asking for advice couched with, "I know I'm the one who has to make the decision but I'd really value your opinion."
- Instead of "You're always on my back," try, "I enjoy being with you more when we don't argue."
- When you reach an impasse: "I'm glad we can disagree and still love each other," or "I know that to you it seems as if I'm making the wrong decision, but to me it's the right one."
- When things with parents hit bottom, having the courage and class to say, "I love you, but visiting you makes me feel unworthy and unloved. I need a month to collect my thoughts. Then we'll try again."

how come i feel so disconnected
if this is such a user-friendly world?

58

The bottom line: to remember that only parents who don't care about their grown children don't have problems with them. Worse than parents who are intrusive are those who don't care enough to care.

Be the glue to help cement the bond between your parents and your children.

Our children are blessed with grandparents who are healthier and living longer, who have more money and more leisure time than any generation before them. Our parents are blessed with grandchildren who, exposed to AIDS, drugs, crime, single-parent households, and dual-career families, have never needed more the unconditional love a grandparent supplies. Both generations might not realize it, but with a little help from us, they'll see that their needs and strengths define a perfect match. If we're the sandwich generation, let's be peanut butter—and make sure the sandwich sticks together.

"My father was frightened by his mother. I was frightened by my father, and I'm damned well going to make sure that my children are frightened of me."

—George V

Staying connected hinges on the time and attention grandparents and grandchildren are willing to give each other. Mutually beneficial relationships will flourish if you encourage your parents and your children to:

- Spend one-on-one time together. When a family gathers, there's little opportunity for individual contact. Alone time—to talk and share intimate secrets—is what creates lifelong memories.

- Dig below the surface. Invest in finding a common interest—a hobby or a sport, a shared concern can become a bridge to build conversation and closeness. Grandparents acting as family historians can enrich their grandchildren's experiences with stories of what life was like when they were young.

- Care about the details going on in each other's lives. Children and grandparents can share favorite TV shows, foods, and pet peeves, as well as personal triumphs and disappointments.

- Keep in regular contact with phone calls, letters, photos, cassettes, or videotapes. Family members can send each other messages, riddles, amusing or interesting newspaper clippings, even anecdotes or bedtime stories on tape.

- Have fun. Splurging on ice cream sodas, giggling at a silly movie, having a sleepover, doing something

Personalizing History

"My father's family is from Denver; my mother is from Newark," says Alice, a mother of two preschoolers who now lives with her family in Rockville, Maryland. "When I had children of my own, I became curious about my roots. I started asking questions, but neither of my parents could answer them. So I started exploring.

"Once I overcame the awkwardness of talking to people I didn't know, I called distant relatives to ask questions about my family. I also began a letter-writing campaign—you have to like writing letters to do any genealogical study.

"I found out I had a great-aunt born in the 1870s who had written in her diary the birth and death dates of her siblings. Her daughter sent me an old address book she found, and I wrote letters to Norway, Italy, and South America. I discovered a relative in Brazil who had a son my age and grandchildren the same ages as my kids. The next time he came to Washington for business, we met, and he brought me an old family album.

"There is an incredible richness in personalizing history. I feel I'm preserving something very precious that would otherwise be lost. My search might have started as wanting to know who I was, but it has almost become an addiction."

how come i feel so disconnected
if this is such a user-friendly world?

60

together that might be met with a frown by mom and dad are guaranteed to cement the bonds between grandparent and grandchild.

- Accept and respect the differences of time and change. Even if grandmas wear sneakers, they might not "get" MTV; even if children are clean, they might be wearing jeans with holes in them. Love and support are not trendy.

- Continue to reinforce their presence in each other's hearts and minds.

You know who you are—but where did you come from? Trace your family roots.

In 1977, when Alex Haley's "Roots" aired on TV, thousands of emotionally moved viewers decided that they too wanted to learn about their ancestors. Since then, genealogy has become one of America's most popular indoor hobbies. Genealogical societies are kept busy assisting people from different ethnic backgrounds who are trying to dig up their roots and climb their family trees.

Through genealogy comes the realization that along with our many differences, we are all of the same origin. By preserving information that might otherwise be lost, we are providing a legacy for the next generation. By looking back, we find inspiration to go forward.

Tracing your family roots is like trying to solve a 10-D puzzle—moving through time and space. Digging for ancestors involves far more than coming up with a collection of names and dates. It's the details of these ancestors' lives that excite and inspire.

Here's how to get started on your own genealogical study:

1. Use what you know.

Begin with the people closest to home—your parents and grandparents. Record as much as you can of the following: full names; dates of major events (birth, baptism, bar mitzvah, marriage, moves, divorce, immigration, language spoken, religion, political affiliation, death, and burials); the towns or countries people lived in; names of their parents, siblings, spouses, and children. Use your family's records and memorabilia, and work toward the unknown.

2. Write, call, or visit relatives—starting with the oldest.

Use a tape recorder or video camera to capture their recollections. Give them advance notice so they can prepare by turning over in their memories tales of people, places, and things. When you visit, take along any old family photographs to help evoke memories.

3. Ask specific questions.

Instead of "Tell me about my great-grandfather," ask, "What was his name? Occupation? Where was he born? Where did he live?"

4. Also ask open-ended questions—the ones that will lead to the most interesting family stories.

Encourage *bobbe-mysehs* (the Yiddish word translates into "old grandmother's story"). These are tales of fighting and survival; stories of courage and enduring hardship; memories of holidays, rituals, and life in "the good old days."

> *"No matter how many communes anybody invents, the family always creeps back."*
>
> —*Margaret Mead*

how come i feel so disconnected
if this is such a user-friendly world?

62

5. Organize.

To be a successful genealogist—and avoid wasting time searching for material you already have—you must be organized. Start with file folders, a loose-leaf notebook that allows notes to be rewritten and discarded, and a hearty supply of envelopes and stamps.

Begin with a lineage chart with your name at the bottom as number 1. Extend lines to number 2 (your father) and number 3 (your mother—use her maiden name). From each of their names, extend lines for their parents and number them. Below each entry, list place and date of birth, marriage, and death. Fill in and extend the chart as more pieces fall together.

Write down every bit of information you learn—even the most unimportant-sounding story. You've seen enough TV whodunits to know that the silliest clue can turn up missing evidence. Treat genealogy as an unsolved mystery and you'll be on your way to solving each problem that arises.

6. Search the attic.

Look for supporting records and papers handed down by your family—letters, notebooks, diaries, scrapbooks, photographs, newspaper clippings, and obituaries—the real gold mines of family facts. Don't discount papers that don't make sense—they may provide invaluable clues as your search progresses.

7. Expand your contacts.

Find out who else in your community is tracing their ancestors and get in touch—usually they'll be willing to pool their experience to help you avoid common pitfalls. Joining a local genealogical or historical society will provide access to records and research advice. If your ancestors lived else-where, join that area's group too—you may discover distant relatives from grandpa's hometown who can supply you with valuable information.

8. Branch out—seek outside sources.

While you are busy interviewing family members and combing through attics, begin to use public records for your research.

9. Be patient; genealogy is a long process.

It will take you months and years to exhaust all possibilities. To get the most satisfaction, remember: there are no rules. You can stop any time or continue your search as an ongoing hobby.

10. Let your research live!

After investing so much time and effort in exploring your family tree, share the fruits of your labor with the rest of your family.[12]

As Sally (see box) and many others who have climbed their family trees know well, knowledge of who we were permits an understanding of who we are and who we want to be.

There are many libraries and historical societies that can help you with your research, no matter what your hometown or ethnic background. Genealogical libraries vary in size, from the tiny Peter

Bringing One's History to Life

Sally, a mother and new grandmother—and amateur genealogist—decided to bring her family's history to life through an album filled with photographs and stories.

"After three years of arduous work— collecting documents and photos, digging up dates and records, receiving letters from long-lost relatives in California and Europe, interviewing cousins and great-aunts and recording their stories—I didn't know what to do with it all. Then the idea of an album came to me, with our family tree on the first page, followed by all the pieces I've collected. It might never be complete, but it's my best attempt at recreating our ancestry— a legacy for my children and their children."

how come i feel so disconnected
if this is such a user-friendly world?

64

Foulger Research Library on Nantucket Island off Cape Cod, Massachusetts, to the huge Mormon or Latter Day Saints Family History Library in Salt Lake City, which houses microfilm and volumes containing over two billion names. But don't expect anyone to do the work for you. Following is a resource list that may prove helpful:

Family History Library
35 Northwest Temple Street
Salt Lake City, UT 84150
801-240-2331

Founded in 1894, this is the world's largest collection of genealogical records—open to the general public at no charge. In the U.S. and 40 foreign countries, over 100 Latter Day Saints agents make arrangements with local archivists and government record keepers to film vital statistics. Call to find the branch nearest you.

The National Archives
National Archives and Records Service
General Services Administration
Washington, DC 20408

Federal records, such as census data, are available through the National Archives—with microfilmed records available at 11 regional archives coast to coast or through interlibrary loan at your local public library.

Daughters of the American Revolution
1776 D Street NW
Washington, DC 20006

The DAR has volumes of cemetery material—who is buried where in cemeteries dating back to colonial days.

New York Genealogical & Biographical Society
122-6 East 58th Street
New York, NY 10022

New England Historic Genealogical Society
101 Newbury Street
Boston, MA 02116

New York Public Library
Genealogy & Local History Division
Fifth Avenue and 42nd Street
New York, NY 10018

Peter Foulger Research Library
Box 1016
Nantucket, MA 02554

Manuscripts, logs, and family histories in this collection are of interest to many people, since it is estimated that millions of Americans are descended from the eleven men who originally settled Nantucket Island in the seventeenth century.[13]

Recognize the importance of celebrating traditional holidays. Be aware of how satisfying the "same old thing" can be.

There's something comforting about the constancy of the calendar. Although we belong to a generation that has broken with many homemaking rites, come holiday time we experience an intense

how come i feel so disconnected
if this is such a user-friendly world?

66

tradition attack. Holidays hit us where we live. We want comfort, security, and food, all served in large enough quantities to make us feel loved.

Twelve months a year we bound down the electronic highway, becoming one-minute managers as we microwave yesterday's pizza for dinner. At holiday times we deserve better. Corporate transfers, empty nests, and retirements might separate us, but the more our lives speed up, the more important our holiday rituals and traditions become. These occasions connect us with our past, define our present, and show us a path to our future.

We asked those we interviewed what holiday traditions they savor most. Here are some of the most treasured:

• "Cooking Christmas dinner for forty—using my grandmother's 70-year-old pots."

• "Snuggling in bed with my daughters every Thanksgiving to watch the parade."

• "The three-day preparation for Passover that begins when my mother moves in and takes over my kitchen. When I was growing up, it used to be my grandmother. We were like soldiers in her army. She gave the orders and we obeyed—chopping, peeling, folding. Last spring when Grandma passed down the title of general, my mom, without missing a beat, started assigning the slicing and peeling to my children."

• "My family's St. Patrick's Day celebrations—when the entire clan gathers in New York. We all go, rain or shine, to the parade down Fifth Avenue, then party all night—eating my mother's Irish stew, singing our favorite family songs, and drinking green beer."

• "Mother's Day has always been our weekend to bring the whole family together from all over the country—no excuses accepted. There are fifty of us—and still growing with new marriages and babies every year. My grandmother's birthday is also in May so everyone comes with a present, making her feel like Queen for the Day. We each bring our favorite dishes that have already become family traditions. And we all know we have to starve for a week before—and of course, a week after!"

Create your own new family rituals that will last well into the 21st century.

For some families, it's more difficult today to maintain long-time traditions and hang on to old rituals. Keeping up with the '90s may require some creativity. Where is it written that families that can't be together at Thanksgiving can't make a holiday out of Arbor Day? Or Groundhog Day? There are more than fifty holidays that color the American calendar with their own set of decorations, games, foods, and rituals. Why not turn one of them into a new annual family holiday?

A New Annual Holiday

"For years we spent Christmas weekend together. But now that our kids are grown and married and have little ones of their own, getting everyone to come home has become a problem. A job transfer sent one son to Indiana; a new husband sent our daughter to Washington, D.C.; retirement brought us to Florida.

"Airfare is at its peak expense during the holiday season, and it's only fair that we share our kids with their in-laws. So we unanimously voted to move our family weekend to the last weekend in January—at least until the grandchildren start school and are restricted by school vacations. Our new annual holiday comes just when we need it most—when we're all suffering from the winter blahs. A dose of Florida sunshine and family togetherness does everybody good."

how come i feel so disconnected
if this is such a user-friendly world?

68

A Long-Distance Ritual

"With our sons away at college and the family apart for the first time for Chanukah, the traditional candle lighting wasn't the same. Loneliness inspired us to come up with a solution that satisfied everybody: now we call both sons on a conference call and light the menorah while everyone chants the blessings together. Since we'll be in three different states every year at this time, it's become our newest family ritual."

• Groundhog Day is February 2—a day connected with weather superstitions. Medieval folk thought that hibernating animals came to the surface on this date to observe the state of the weather. Over the years groundhog clubs have sprouted—purely for fun. Your family too can fight the post-Christmas blues with a groundhog club of your own and a yearly winter celebration.

• April Fool's Day is April 1—the day of the year consecrated to practical joking. It's long been a worldwide custom for fun makers to celebrate on All Fool's Day. Perhaps your family can turn an April Fool's party into a yearly family fun-fest.

• Arbor Day—a day devoted to tree planting. The time of year varies in different places, but most observe a date in March or April. The holiday plays an important role in calling attention to the need for conserving our natural resources. Your kids will probably plant trees at school for the enjoyment of future generations. Share the spirit and start a family tree-planting tradition—with accompanying festivities.

• May Day is May 1—the spring festival to honor Flora, the goddess of flowers. It's a time of merrymaking—dancing around the decorated Maypole, playing games, celebrating the onset of spring.

Ever think about an annual May Day festival—choosing someone different in the extended family each year to be the honored May queen?

• Kids' Day is the fourth Saturday in September—sponsored by Kiwanis International and observed in thousands of communities in the U.S. and Canada. Its purpose: to honor youth. The emphasis is on recreation and entertainment; families or communities may gather for field days, picnics, or trips to the movies, amusement parks, rodeos, ball games, or sports events. Families can create their own unique versions of Kids' Day—honoring, appreciating, and enjoying their children and each other.

• United Nations Day is October 24—reason enough to celebrate with an international feast. Choose a different country for the theme each year, or mix and match. When you add decorations, games, and the traditional activities of the chosen nationality, any feast becomes a festival!

• Halloween is October 31—if you're superstitious, it's the night when frustrated ghosts play tricks on humans and cause supernatural happenings. It's an occasion that brings out the fun in all of us and a perfect time for a family masquerade or block party.[14]

When holidays aren't as joyous as they once were, rethink your definition of family.

Holidays can be especially lonely times for people who are single, alone, or recovering from a loss. Their pain and hurt is often magnified by holiday hype. But holidays can in fact enable both healing and cel-

how come i feel so disconnected
if this is such a user-friendly world?

70

Their Own Family Day

"Mother's Day was wonderful until our son's divorce. Then our grandchildren weren't with us anymore on that weekend in May. Father's Day became equally depressing after my father died. So we decided to celebrate our own Family Day, on the first Sunday in June, midway between the traditional holidays. It's been three years now of uniting the troops for a pig-out barbecue and gift exchange, and everybody agrees that this was a great idea."

ebration. The starting place is acknowledging that this year's holidays will be different because they are impacted by change—the death of a loved one, a divorce, or children grown and moved away. Now this time can be used to honor the memory of a family member or to celebrate a family change, a new stage of life, or a new beginning.

If you're facing life changes during holiday time, you might:

• Look to your network of friends and relatives to help organize and share the holidays. Extend your definition of family to include those separated from their families, and forge a new sense of security—reinforced with kindness, compassion, and generosity.

• Rework the holidays to fit the strengths and resources of your current family.

• Incorporate new traditions and create new rituals with your newly defined family. Break away from situations that rekindle memories tinged with regret and sadness.

• Pay attention to what you need. Pamper yourself with something totally self-indulgent to brighten up an otherwise gloomy holiday.

• Put a boundary around tensions or ongoing conflicts so they don't directly intrude on holiday time. Give everyone a protected time and space to enjoy special events together.

• Use small ways to help kids regain some control when a parent is missing from the holiday table. This may mean making contact with the absent parent or, if that's impossible, having an honest discussion about the unique strengths of your newly redefined family.

• Remind yourself not to place too much emphasis on one particular 24-hour period. After all, it's the daily celebrations of life that count much more.[15]

Be in charge of organizing a family reunion. Build a family identity for the future.

If you're inspired to add your family to the more than 200,000 families who hold an annual reunion, there's plenty of work ahead. Here's how to get started:

1. Plan ahead.

Nine months to a year in advance is the recommended preparation time for a first-time reunion. Begin by defining your family unit. Then compile a mailing list and send a preliminary flyer to see who's interested; which dates are most convenient; how much participants are willing to pay for lodging, food, and incidentals; and who can help with the planning. A tear-off section at the bottom of the letter makes it easy for people to reply.

2. Choose the place.

Does anyone in the family own a home with a big backyard? Is there a public park located near someone's house? Would your family prefer to gather at a hotel? At a dude ranch? On a cruise ship?

how come i feel so disconnected
if this is such a user-friendly world?

72

The Right Strangers Can Also Be Thicker Than Water!

"Our first Thanksgiving as a married couple was a major disappointment," confesses Alex. *"My ex-wife had my kids; Paula's son was off skiing with his father. My parents were in Florida, and Paula's mother was too weak to leave the nursing home. So the next year we carefully planned in advance. Our Thanksgiving table became a haven for strays—our new neighbors who had just relocated 2,000 miles from their hometown, Paula's single cousin, our newly divorced friend and her two teenage sons, and my gay friend Howie.*

"At first it was awkward sitting around the table with a group of strangers, but it's amazing what a big turkey meal can do! By the end of the evening, Paula's cousin and Howie had discovered a mutual passion for ballet and were contemplating taking a season subscription together, our friend's 16-year-old son found a fellow Knicks fanatic to compare basketball statistics with, and the mood couldn't have been livelier and warmer if we were flesh and blood."

After collecting the responses from your mailing, be sure that, wherever you decide to hold the reunion, there's a central area where participants can congregate, a space appropriate for informal activities, room for the kids to run around, and adequate parking. If family members are traveling a distance and plan to spend a night or two, check out the local hotels for prices and availability.

3. Spread the word.

Once you've chosen the place and date, send out a second announcement. Any deposit required? Include a list of missing relatives, and ask for information about their whereabouts. An RSVP phone number with a deadline date is a must.

4. Use a team approach to work out the details.

Recruit a committee to make this a family affair. Responsibilities should be shared. Who will keep a count of who's coming?

Who will keep track of expenses and collect any cash? Who's in charge of reservations? The menu? Paper goods?

5. Plan activities to provide structure.

While you don't want to fill every minute, activities are fun and offer opportunities to mingle and get acquainted. A "family minutes" session is a good introduction: a brief time during which relatives announce any important personal news they wish to share. Other activity ideas might be a family Olympics with teams of mixed generations, a talent show, or perhaps a theme party for evening fun—karaoke, western, or Las Vegas night.

6. Find a way to record the reunion.

Some families establish a family archive, where recordings and memorabilia are stored. Others plan a special project to commemorate the reunion. How about a family album filled with rediscovered old letters, newspaper clippings, and photos? Or a more current album? Mementos, like a reunion T-shirt with a design featuring the family name, help keep the memory of the occasion alive. Call on relatives with special equipment and talents to take photos, videotape the event, or make oral history tapes.

7. Review the reunion to make the next one even better.

At some point, near the end of the reunion or with a follow-up afterward, evaluate what worked and what didn't. Decide who will organize the next one and pass on the previous planner's notes and materials. Anything that went wrong can be a lesson for the future—for sure it'll be what people remember and share at the next reunion![16]

"Home is not where you live but where they understand you."
—*Christian Morgenstern*

how come i feel so disconnected
if this is such a user-friendly world?

74

• CLOSING THOUGHTS

A medieval legend tells of a man who was incarcerated in the dungeon of his enemy's castle. While the frustration of imprisonment at first seemed unbearable, he gradually adjusted to his wretched existence. For twenty long years he rotted in loneliness, seeing no one, not even the guard who pushed his food through the bottom of the cell door.

And then one day, as the prisoner was pacing about his cell, he absentmindedly stopped at the door and turned the knob. There was a squeaking of ancient hinges as the huge portal slowly opened before the startled old man. "My heavens," thought the aged prisoner. "The door was unlocked all the time and I never had the sense to try it."

If the world of Hallmark holiday celebrations and heartwarming reunions seems closed to you, make sure you're not trapped in a prison cell of your own making. If contact with your brothers and sisters and older parents is unsatisfyingly distant, check to see that you're not wasting valuable days and years waiting for them to do your work and open an unlocked door.

The truth is that no one can open up the door to your heart but yourself. Your branch on the family tree is inscribed. Pay it some attention and watch it bloom.

chapter four

"With You I Don't Have to Be All Things ... Just Me"

Forging Honest, Loving, Just Friends

"If we all were given by magic the power to read each other's thoughts, I suppose the first effect would be to dissolve all friendships."
—Bertrand Russell

how come i feel so disconnected
if this is such a user-friendly world?

76

F riends demand a lot from us. They ask for advice, sympathy, and compassion. They need to be supported, encouraged, and forgiven. But if we supply a friend with what he needs, we will have, without written contract or legal pledge, a reliable, everlasting, unbreakable connection. Friends strengthen not only our self-image and our spirit but our hearts as well. A half-dozen medical studies agree that spending satisfying time with friends helps us ward off depression, boosts our immune system, increases the odds of surviving coronary disease, and can even extend our life expectancy.[1] The triple *A* of benefits enjoyed in intimate friendships—acceptance, affirmation, and affection—form a support system that is powerful medicine.

Unfortunately, the price of "making it" in the '90s too often relegates friendship to secondary status. We forget that as children we were judged on our ability to make and keep friends. The stigma and shame of the times we failed make up our most miserable childhood memories. As parents, there's no greater gift we can wish for our kids than the satisfaction and security of honest, long-lasting, laughter-filled friendships. And we must be reminded, in these hectic times, to show by example that friendships deserve the same nurturing and attention we give our families.

Because they're easier to fit in, it's the friendships nourished by proximity that often wind up as our most intimate. We talk to the man who sits next to us on the train and the woman on the next treadmill . . . because they're there. We have to work harder to give our "bestest" friends—the ones we don't bump into without conscious effort—the time their loyalty has earned. And while sometimes we might be lucky in love, in our friendships we get what we give. All we have to do is look at the tremendous satisfaction teenagers derive from their friends, giving them the time and attention they deserve, to see what's ours for the taking.

Thankfully, our friends are a hardy lot and are used to surviving periods of neglect. They too have family celebrations, business obligations, community commitments, professional command performances, and lives that are as crowded with "shoulds" and "have-tos" as ours. They too are aware that as small as the world might be getting, it's still rare to find a person you can tell the truth to, a person who will tell you if there's something on your nose or you have lipstick on your teeth, a person who thinks you're uniquely "hot stuff." We owe ourselves the time to make memories with our friends.

> *"Promises may get friends, but it is performance that must nurse and keep them."*
>
> *—Owen Feltham*

• TRIED AND TRUE

What are the most important factors in staying connected with our friends? Is it how often we see them, talk to them, play with them—or something more? There have been almost as many love songs written about friendship as there have been about romantic love. The yearning for a sidekick, a buddy—someone who will keep life events in perspective and replenish our sense of connectedness—is universal. When we asked those we surveyed, "What comes to mind when you think of intimate friendship?"—these were some of the responses:

how come i feel so disconnected
if this is such a user-friendly world?

78

- "The opportunity to be unconditionally accepted, even at your worst"
- "An anchor, a person you can trust to be committed to your best interests"
- "Someone who shares your attitudes and values, and who also appreciates what makes you one of a kind"
- "A place you can go and not only not be judged, but be protected from those who might judge you"
- "A person with the unique ability to just listen and, without saying a word, make you feel better"
- "A human being you can whine 'why me?' to, who won't think less of you"
- "A relationship fueled by shared confidences, real honesty, and frequent loud laughter"
- "An acceptor of a sincere apology who'll forgive any selfishness, greed, ignorance, or cruelty"
- "A sounding board who'll take the time to consider your problem and then offer wise advice"
- "Someone whose presence alone, because they've stood by you through all the years and all the changes, is remedy enough to bolster shaky self-confidence"

Use the various compartments of your life to expand your friendships. Gather ye friendships wherever ye can.

Friendships can be conducted on many levels of intensity. They serve different functions, meet different needs, and range from the most spiritual of soulmates to the most nonchalant and casual of buddies.

We grew up with a narrower definition—a friend was one who hated everything you hated, loved everyone you loved, and kept no secrets from you. Today we cheat ourselves if we don't take advantage of the various cubbyholes of life to warm and nourish ourselves with a more flexible definition of friendship.

While not all of the following relationships are intimate, all can be rewarding.

"If our paths didn't cross, we'd never be friends." This cubbyhole includes the people we see all the time, not because of who they are but because of where they live. Hours are spent next to those with whom we ride the train, get manicures, and exercise. We have relationships with the parents of our children's friends and those with whom we share a street address. These are people we exchange favors with, not secrets. They know where we work, but not how much money we make; how many years we've been married, but not how many were spent unhappily.

"I like New York in June, how about you?" Then there are those friends who have similar passions. In these relationships it's the "doing" together, not the "being" together, that's their strength. Poker games and basketball, book clubs and tennis, Cancer Care and the NRA make playmates, if not soulmates, out of strangers.

"Those were the days, my friend." Friends we laugh at and with, with the most respect and the least awe, are those who knew us when—the old friends with whom we share a unique history. They

how come i feel so disconnected
if this is such a user-friendly world?

80

are the friends we might have little in common with now, but who remind us of a part of ourselves we don't want to lose. They are the ones we look to hug when a parent dies, and those to whom we can't wait to tell gossip about the old neighborhood. Because they are an intimate connection to our past, they are forever in our hearts.

"I haven't seen you in fourteen hours, what's up?" No relationship includes as many daily details—every cavity, every late payment, every Little League score—as a workplace friendship. But what we mostly talk about is the office. When one moves on, however, there's not much left if the friendship hasn't taken root outside the workplace.

> *"I love everything that's old: old friends, old times, old manners, old books, old wines . . . and old friends are the best!"*
> *—Oliver Goldsmith*

"Where would we be without our better half?" We never see these friends alone—only as part of a couple at couples' parties. Although we share interests, there's not enough time or motivation to deepen the relationship one-on-one. Yet it's always fun to spend an evening together, and its pleasure quotient qualifies it as a friendship. But if you divorce or move away, don't expect anything long lasting.

"Go figure!" The last category includes mystical connections that defy all the rules. One wife of twenty years and mother of three says, "My friend is single, independent, and funky. I thrive on lists, love to stay home, and sleep with a watch. Jill is game to try anything, is always planning her next adventure, and never knows what time it is. We know each other's favorite foods, favorite colors, and favorite authors—though we share not one."

These friendships are not defined by growing up together or working together or living on the same block or working for the same cause, but they are friendships in the richest sense of the word. What defines them may be a mutual admiration or a sharing of each other's intuitive "getting" of who we are at our very core.

Do not expect of your adult friends what you took for granted in your childhood friends.

The road to long-lasting friendship is littered with the dashed expectations of the 12-year-old inside us. Cast away those immature myths of friendship:

Myth #1. *A true friend shares everything in common with me.* Although many people audition for closeness throughout our lives, we reward only a few with the part. As children, we chose friends with whom we shared every taste and every opinion. As adults, we see the value of trading off commonality for the differences that give us experiences to exchange.

Myth #2. *Real friends tell each other everything.* Twelve-year-olds tell each other everything; wise adults learn that letting it all hang out—total honesty—can lead to arguments and hurt feelings.

"What will it accomplish?" is a good question to ask before turning your connection into a collision. If the answer is, "It'll make me feel

"Don't flatter yourself that friendship authorizes you to say disagreeable things to your intimates. The nearer you come into relation with a person, the more necessary do tact and courtesy become. Except in cases of necessity, which are rare, leave your friend to learn unpleasant things from his enemies; they are ready enough to tell him."
—*Oliver Wendell Holmes*

how come i feel so disconnected
if this is such a user-friendly world?

82

better at the price of driving a wedge in our friendship,"—write it down, stick it in a night table, and go on.

Myth #3. *A good friend always knows what I need.* Psychic powers that reveal when a friend needs more attention or more space, some sympathy, or a kick in the butt also dissipate in adolescence. As adults, we have to use language clearly and directly if we want our friends to satisfy our needs. Expecting to be soothed by a friend who hasn't been told you're hurting leads to totally predictable, totally avoidable disappointment.

Myth #4. *My friends are more important to me when I'm down and out.* A friend in need is a friend indeed—but where are you when I get a promotion? We have to realize the unhappy truth that friends find it easier to be our saviors when we're down than to be our cheerleaders when we're flying high. We must be vigilant in canning our envy and being effusive in expressing our delight when good things happen to our friends.

Myth #5. *Good friendships never have crises.* George Washington once said, "True friendship must undergo and withstand the shocks of adversity before it is entitled to the appellation of friendship." Crises in honest, long-lasting relationships are unavoidable; surviving them proves we are worthy of our friends.

Myth #6. *A good friend will never betray me.* Sometimes even soulmates commit the terrorism of friendship: betrayal. Whether a betrayal is unintentional or a misunderstanding, it hurts just the same. But before you pronounce a relationship deceased:

1. Put yourself in your friend's shoes; give your friend the benefit of the doubt.

2. Ask for an explanation without accusing or attacking.

3. If you're still troubled after the explanation, be honest and tell your friend how you feel.

4. Try to forgive and forget. Dwelling on one incident of betrayal will only keep you from trusting. If you can, let the incident go. If it was too serious to forgive, try giving yourself some time away from that friend, leaving the door open for reconciliation at a later time. Friends make mistakes. Don't compound them by sacrificing a relationship that might be salvageable.[2]

Start a tradition together–and make it last.

Why do some friendships fizzle away while others survive—and thrive—over decades? One factor, psychologists agree, is continuity; friends who create rituals and traditions together and remain committed to keeping them—weekly, monthly, even yearly—contribute positive energy to their connection.

It could be the littlest thing. For instance, Sandy and Denise have been food shopping together every Sunday morning for five years. "We both work and never get to see each other," says Sandy. "Since each of us did our grocery shopping on Sundays, we came up with this great idea: why not meet at a supermarket midway between us and walk the aisles together? Now we have a chance to catch up on a week's worth of gossip. The store's never crowded, and we finish fast, even giving ourselves the gift of a cup of coffee afterward, before it's time for Sunday School carpools."

It could be something based on a common interest or pursuit. Carol and Joan decided to volunteer at their local hospital together

how come i feel so disconnected
if this is such a user-friendly world?

84

one afternoon a week. For more than a year they've been spending their Wednesdays sharing not only lunch and on-the-job anecdotes at the hospital coffee shop, but the unbeatable feeling of gratification that comes with giving.

Or maybe it's a special time to look forward to. Bruce and Danny have been spending July 4th together for twenty years—a tradition they started in college. "Nothing was going to get in our way," insists Bruce. "By the time we both got married, it was a ritual set in stone. Our wives could either join us or be left behind. A barbecue and fireworks—how could they resist?"

Similarly, Jill and Bob and Kenny and Marsha met on their honeymoons and have been vacationing together ever since. One couple from Michigan, the other from Delaware, they've been meeting during the second week of February for the past eight years.

"We've gone to the Caribbean, skiing in Vermont, and to a few hotels in the Poconos," says Marsha. "It's not as important where we go as that we're together for that week. In between, we try to grab a weekend here and there, but with two kids each, it's not always possible. At least we have those seven days to look forward to—no matter what."

It's hard work today to fight excuses and exhaustion and to be tougher than the many reasons we have to give in to "Oh well, we tried." But special rituals between friends are worth fighting for. Those patterns set in the '90s—with the help of continuity and commitment—can seal friendships well into the 21st century.

Whether they're called buddies or soulmates, respect how the opposite gender "befriends."

Our gender patterns may date back to the time of when we lived in caves. Anthropologist Helen Fischer offers this age-old explanation: The cavemen, who went out scavenging side by side, had to keep quiet or they'd scare off their prey. Consequently, they became close by doing. Their women were gatherers and stayed in one place. Face-to-face conversation kept prey away and was an important part of their interaction. They became close by "being."[3]

In each of the following pairs, compare the genders and the way they define their friendships. Would that the rest of life were as easy to decipher. . . .

- A. A friend is someone to go out with and have fun with.
- B. A friend is someone to trust and confide in.

- A. They talk about sports, cars, politics, and sex.
- B. They talk about kids, having kids, marriage, their jobs, their mothers, their fathers, relationships, thoughts, feelings, fantasies, fears, politics, and sex.

She Said, He Said . . .

"Men don't smell the flowers when they get together; they count them," said a woman we spoke to, comparing her husband's conversations with her own. "How can a discussion about the biggest fish and the lowest golf score possibly rival in richness a conversation about our fathers and how we all realized we forgave them anything if we were sure they loved us?"

And from her husband: "Chit-chat, yak-yak, dissect, burrow in, and explore—my wife and her friends can talk for hours. My friends and I don't have to open a vein and bleed to feel close. Women can't understand: it's not that we're repressing or afraid to be vulnerable . . . we just don't need what they need. Our contact is more sporadic and less intense, but it works for us. And we're not into betraying our wives' trust by repeating every word of our latest argument."

how come i feel so disconnected
if this is such a user-friendly world?

86

A. They exchange public news.

B. They exchange private news.

A. They trade war stories.

B. They trade the truth about themselves.

A. They bond at bars, football stadiums, basketball courts, and gyms.

B. They bond in living rooms, dining rooms, dens, and kitchens.

A. They become close by doing.

B. They become close by being.

A. "My son scored 14 points in the basketball game yesterday!"

B. "My son seemed distracted on the court yesterday; I wonder what's on his mind."

A. "What do you think went wrong with the Dallas Cowboys?"

B. "What do you think went wrong with our relationship?"

A. There are friends for different purposes; there are friends and there are friends.

B. Friends are holistic; a friend is a friend.

Do we have to tell you which is which?

Use the $1.7 billion greeting card industry to express what's too tough to say to your friends.[4]

Because we've become so transient (one in six of us moves every year) and walk around tired, overworked, and often stressed, it's more difficult today than ever before to maintain close friendships.[5]

The phone and fax are adequate for communicating information, but when it comes to messages of support and reassurance, expressions of anxiety and irritation, or outpourings of our deeply felt private thoughts, written communication does it best. American ingenuity has expanded the role of the "happy birthday people" to include lines of nonoccasion greeting cards to say what we wish we'd said.

If you can't write the note yourself or open up in a face-to-face conversation, then just sign your name to a chatty, meaningful sentiment written for you—and thousands like you. Accept the help. If a friend's dog dies, if you need to apologize for a bad mood, if you want to express concern for a friend with a drinking problem—invest in a card and a stamp. A few minutes' effort lets someone you care about know you're thinking of them.

The two most popular situations in need of card-generated speeches are "to support a friend who's having a rough time emotionally" and the old standby, "to tell a friend he's special and say how much you care."[6]

Appreciate your work friendships . . . and learn to recognize their appropriate place in your life.

For many of us, our work pals are the only friends we have time for these days. Since the mid-1970s, Americans have been spending more and more time at the office; in fact, after work, chores, sleep, and commuting, we have only 17 free hours a week.[7] Often we're so exhausted it's difficult to muster up the energy—or motivation—to socialize with "real-world" friends.

how come i feel so disconnected
if this is such a user-friendly world?

88

Work Friendships Have Their Own Perks

On-the-job friends can supply camaraderie, spirit, and fun to help make going to work every morning more pleasant.

- A "100 Maple Avenue Softball League" was the creation of two friends whose companies shared the same office building. One day at lunch in the cafeteria, they came up with the idea, which was so well received by their coworkers that by the end of the day two coed teams of ten had been formed. Within a week, six other offices joined the league, with games scheduled at a local park Tuesday evenings. Here was an opportunity to share a common goal, with colleagues united in a way that cut through petty office tensions and blurred the distinction between labor and management.

- Monthly Pep Breakfasts combat the isolation of working from home for three freelance writers who met at a local conference. They trade ideas and suggestions for their latest projects, commiserate over writer's blocks, applaud each other's accomplishments, and contribute a dose of much-needed inspiration to keep them going till next month's meeting.

- The Betting Pool was the idea of four coworkers in an office. "Every Friday we each throw $5 in a pot for the weekly bet," explains Rick, one of the quartet. "The winner takes home $20. The rule is that all bets are trivial. We've bet on what the cafeteria's yogurt flavor of the day will be, or the time our boss would mosey into work—the closest pick won. It's no big deal, but it makes Fridays fun."

As the office becomes our community and our work friends become more important than ever, they often know more about our day-to-day lives than our spouses or kids. Sometimes we're lucky enough to discover special relationships through work that carry over to the weekends. These are friendships based on support and trust, in which partners share not only common interests, but also mistakes, doubts, and concerns. Other relationships, as comfortable and easy as they may seem while at work, may be just that—office friendships.

The trick is to be able to recognize the difference between seven-day-a-week friendships and those that work better left within the confines of the workplace. If you can accept—and appreciate—the variety among your office friendships, you'll find both kinds can be rewarding.

To nurture your work relationships, Long Island, New York, psychologist Dr. Michael Peltzman suggests:

• Let your work friends know how important they are to you. Be liberal with affirmation and praise.

• Develop rituals together—lunch out every Friday, a coffee break at 10:30, weekly office pools for football games. Constancy reinforces the bonds of workplace friendships.

• Pursue interests with your work pals that are unrelated to the job. Take a course together, join a gym, volunteer in a community project. Sharing activities is a good way to strengthen relationships.

• Schedule breaks for conversation during work. If the workplace is busy and noisy and your own assignments require your undivided attention, set aside time for non-work-related dialogue. A five-minute break at the vending machines to catch up on personal news is an instant pick-me-up.

• Develop a network with your workplace friends that encourages mutual self-interest. Reciprocate favors to make each other's jobs easier or promote success.

• Be cautious with criticism. Before you speak your mind, ask yourself, "Will this accomplish a positive change?" Remember, after you speak, you'll still have to face your friend every day at the office.

And a few tips in self-defense:

how come i feel so disconnected
if this is such a user-friendly world?

90

> *"The meeting of two personalities is like the contact of two chemical substances; if there is any reaction, both are transformed."*
>
> —*Carl Jung*

- Beware of disclosing job-related mistakes or incidents that might make you appear unstable or unreliable to coworkers who are competing with you and could be tempted to use this information.

- Keep in contact with friends who move to different departments or other companies. Leave your options open with connections that can help you if you ever leave your job.

- If a work friend becomes the boss—don't try to leverage the friendship for special favors. To help continue the friendship smoothly, talk honestly and openly about the awkwardness of the situation. And whenever possible, try to treat it with a sense of humor.

Fight clean with your friends. The way we handle conflicts can either ruin our friendships or deepen them.

With time and energy at a premium, it's tempting to take what appears to be the easy way out and let things slide. But friendship is too precious a commodity to leave to chance. Our friends—and our problems with them—deserve our undivided attention.

Alan Loy McGinnis, author of *The Friendship Factor,* says that fighting clean is not only possible but essential in solid friendships. He offers five techniques for clean fighting.

Talk about your feelings—not your friend's faults. Instead of going for the jugular, take responsibility for your own feelings. Not:

"You never pay attention to me anymore," but "I'm feeling very lonely these days." Instead of "You never . . ." or "You always . . ." try, "I'm upset because . . . ," "I get bugged when . . . ," "I wish you would . . . ," or "I'd really appreciate it if. . . ."

Stick to one topic. Don't let past grievances surface to cloud the issue at hand, but, instead, deal with one situation at a time. Are you angry with a friend who didn't call you after you had surgery? Address this disappointment only—not other unresolved problems you've been collecting over the past two years.

Allow your friend to respond. What sometimes seems like a knock-down-drag-out session may in fact be the healthiest kind of fighting—taking turns expressing anger and listening to the other side. People who walk out during an argument are dirty fighters, says Dr. McGinnis. If you're angry with a friend, express those feelings; then stick around to listen, while keeping the doors open for resolution or compromise.

Aim for ventilation—not conquest. The goal is not always to win but to get out pent-up hostility and anger. Some of the best and cleanest fights have no winner and no surrender but end with both partners feeling cleansed and rejuvenated.

But when you know you're wrong—apologize. Apologizing is not a form of weakness; it takes strength to admit when you're wrong. Norman Vincent Peale wrote, "A true apology is more than just acknowledgment of a mistake. It is recognition that something you

how come i feel so disconnected
if this is such a user-friendly world?

92

have said or done has damaged a relationship—and that you care enough about the relationship to want it repaired and restored."

Reality Check–Among Friends

The big new trend in comedy on TV the last few years is shows about friends. On the surface, the plots concern themselves with nothing more than sitting around talking about nothing—one of the prerequisite ingredients in a committed friend relationship! Here are some statistics on the bond that most quickly brings out the best and worst in us:

- Up to 45 percent of us name one or more neighbors among our three closest friends.
- Fewer than four out of ten Americans have a close friend of a different race. Less than 50 percent have a close friend from a different ethnic group.
- More than half of all friends are less than five years apart in age.
- More than 20 percent of us have known our dearest friend for twenty years or more.
- Ninety percent of women and 75 percent of men have "had an intimate talk" in the last month.
- The most important attributes of a friend are considered to be loyalty and the ability to keep a secret.
- Ninety-seven percent of Americans have friends whom they label as "close" but whom they do not see regularly.
- The number-one reason for a strained friendship is betrayal.[8]

Balance criticism with affection. No matter how difficult it is for us to hear that we've disappointed, angered, or hurt a friend, the words are easier to tolerate if couched with a hug, some other affectionate gesture, or affirmation that we are important and the friendship special.

When you're on the criticizing end, try softening the edges with: "You know how much you mean to me, but it really hurt me when you lied about . . ." or "Since I consider you my best friend, I'm especially angry that you violated my confidence when you didn't keep my secret about. . . ." Remember: you can fight clean with expressions of anger if you balance them with expressions of love.[9]

Remove the dead wood of your friendships from your social calendar.

Making new friends and losing touch with others is a natural consequence of growing up and older. Friends tend to talk about and share the most important experiences of their lives, so, as experiences change, the need for new friends develops. Old friends sometimes coast for years on a reputation earned decades earlier. We often think friendships are so precious that it's our duty to try to work things out and save them. That's true for the ones that work.

But when a friendship undermines our self-esteem and even contributes to our feelings of disconnectedness, it's time to reevaluate. The childhood friends whose identities formed as ours did will not necessarily answer the friendship needs of today. It's awkward but necessary to periodically scrutinize our bonds to determine which are still strong.

As good for the soul as good friends are, the hostility and anger that unsatisfactory relationships incur can be damaging. Realizing that a friendship no longer works gives us the time and motivation to develop new friendships that better affirm our self-image.

If you doubt the support you're getting from an old friend, ask yourself:

how come i feel so disconnected
if this is such a user-friendly world?

94

- Does he/she accept me unconditionally?
- How often lately has he/she made me feel special and unique?
- Is he/she as affectionate toward me today as in the past?

If the answer to these questions is no, and you've done your best to hold up your end of the friendship, it may be time to end it and move on.

Nurture your friendships, and they will last a lifetime.

Friendship is not an instinct. Like the relationships between husbands and wives, parents and children, and brothers and sisters, strong friendships require a steady effort.

According to pollster Daniel Yankelovich, 70 percent of Americans say they have many acquaintances but few close friends and that they see this as a serious void in their lives.[10] Too many of us have mistakenly believed that friendship is unconditional, and that, because Carole King promised, "winter, spring, summer or fall, all you have to do is call . . . ," we could afford to ignore the upkeep of those who bail us out and prop us up, tell us the best jokes, and have the most comfortable shoulders to lean on.

There are lots of ways to cement your friendships and keep them strong.

Make friends a priority. Make sure there's time to spend together. It doesn't have to be a whole afternoon or even dinner. According to Steven Duck, author of *Friends for Life,* talks that matter most tend to last only a few minutes. It's not the discussions of the meaning of life that show friends you care; it's the good-luck call before a stressful presentation, an inquiry about your wisdom tooth, a note of congratulation on a recent achievement, that keep a friendship going.[11]

Be friend-centered, not self-centered. This means giving up something of yourself for the other person, so that the person feels valued. It can mean going out of your way, listening when you'd rather not, or doing things for a friend when you have little time to get your own stuff done. It's a small price to pay for a reliable, dependable safety net when times get hairy.

Risk being yourself. If you resist opening up because you're afraid that if your friends see your flaws they'll like you less, you're not trusting enough. It can be endearing to admit your faults, fears, disappointments, and negative emotions, and your honesty will allow your friends the same luxury.

> *"We inherit our relatives and our features and may not escape them; but we can select our clothing and our friends, and let us be careful that both fit us."*
> —*Volney Streamer*

Respect each other's individuality. Strong friendships enjoy the right mixture of commonality and difference. Most friends have enough in common to understand each other and enough difference so that there's something spicy to exchange.

Let your friends be generous. It's important to let your friends know you need them. Just as you feel happy to help a friend, give your friend a chance to help you. It sounds almost too good to be true: "If you want a man to be a friend, ask him to do you a favor."

how come i feel so disconnected
if this is such a user-friendly world?

96

> *"When my friends lack an eye, I look at them in profile."*
>
> —*Joseph Joubert*

Don't let geographical distance or time constraints be a barrier to remaining close. To nurture long-distance friendships, visit as often as possible, make long-distance dates to get together for coffee over the phone, send audiotapes or videotapes back and forth to "visit" without leaving home, correspond regularly by mail, or go the modern route: If you have access to a computer, send easy instant e-mail messages to each other.

• ARE YOU A GOOD FRIEND?

No one deserves your best more than the best of your friends. Keep these vital connections healthy by making their upkeep a priority. Judge the job you're doing by seeing how many of these questions you can answer with a truthful "Yes."

1. Do you assign a high priority to your friendships?

2. Are you open enough with your friends to allow them to see what's in your heart?

3. Are you a good listener?

4. Are you willing to accept your friends' imperfections?

5. Do you show affection to your friends?

6. Are you generous with your friends—giving your time and effort, without expecting anything in return?

7. Do you stand by your friends as surely when they're down and out as when they're celebrating triumph?

8. Do you communicate your expectations and let your friends know what you need from them?

9. Do you work through crises in your friendships by fighting clean and balancing your expressions of anger with expressions of love?

10. If a friend lets you down, can you forgive and forget?

• CLOSING THOUGHTS

We know it when we feel it: loneliness instantly dissolves as friendship approaches. People from Aristotle to Martin Buber, Plato to Bob Dylan have attempted to define their unique experiences.

Webster says that friendship occurs when "one is attached to another by esteem, respect and affection." While the dictionary defines the word, it does not describe the experience of being a friend. Since every source we consulted on friendship was full of the ways others have described their own relationships, we join them and offer some of the ones that touched us most.

> *We need old friends to help us grow old and new friends to help us stay young.* —Letty Cottin Pogrebin

> *The bird a nest, the spider a web, man friendship.* —William Blake

> *'Stay' is a charming word in a friend's vocabulary.* —Amos Bronson Alcott

> *The costliness of keeping friends does not lie in what one does for them but in what one, out of consideration for them, refrains from doing.* —Henrik Ibsen

how come i feel so disconnected
if this is such a user-friendly world?

98

Nothing is more common than to talk of a friend; nothing more difficult than to find one; nothing more rare than to improve by one as we ought. —Robert Hall

Oh the comfort, the inexpressible comfort of feeling safe with a person: having neither to weigh thoughts or measure words, but to pour them out. Just as they are—chaff and grain together, knowing that a faithful hand will take and sift them, keep what is worth keeping, and then with the breath of kindness, blow the rest away. —George Eliot

I need all the friends I can get. —Charlie Brown

chapter five

"Sign Me Up; I Want to Belong"

Becoming a Contributing Member of Your Community

"We make our friends; we make our enemies; but God makes our next door neighbor."
—G. K. Chesterton

how come i feel so disconnected
if this is such a user-friendly world?

100

There's a tendency in the '90s to believe that if our houses don't have front porches or large windows to keep an eye on what's happening in the street, our sense of community is in trouble. We've read that because our sidewalks are no longer wide, tree-shaded, and full of people, our neighborhoods are inferior to what they once were. The words too often used to describe the communities in which we live—fearful, decaying, fragmented, transitory, superficial—are alarming and misleading. If we're not careful, they could lead us to buy into the myth that the best of stable, satisfying communal life died with Norman Rockwell. If the streets are deserted, it doesn't mean neighbors aren't borrowing power drills and rug shampooers; if we keep up by phone rather than by meeting in public spaces, it doesn't mean we're buying fewer Girl Scout cookies or caring less about each other. Even if dependence on our neighborhood has lessened as social, physical, and economic mobility has increased, our innate need to be participating members of a community has not changed. Community still gives us identity. Neighbors still supply companionship, support, and a helping hand.

But because there's less opportunity for casual neighborly contact today, we need to be reminded to push ourselves—to telephone and invite and attend. While the densely knit "Our Town" of years past was more local, it was not necessarily more noble. Cars and phones now offer us the advantage of networking with people beyond those with whom we rub shoulders. We can use this redefined neighborhood as a secure base from which to engage with the outside world. No matter how large and distant and sterile the world might appear, a shared identity fostered by a sense of community can deal with it.

There is an old story of a father who told his son to use all of his strength to remove a boulder from the road on which they were walking. Try as he might, the little boy couldn't move the rock an inch. "Are you sure that you're using all of the strength that you've got?" the father asked. The child mustered all of his energy but still couldn't move the rock. "You're not using all of your strength," reproved the father. "What more strength do I have?" asked the exhausted son. To which the father answered, "You have my strength—all you have to do is ask for it!"

"Nice to Meet You, Neighbor!"

Paula and Bob were first attracted to their neighborhood by the beauty and privacy of the wooded properites. But their one-acre plot distanced them from their neighbors. Their solution: to organize a neighborhood Olympics party.

Paula, Bob, and their kids dropped invitations into the 25 mailboxes in their development. As each family responded, they were asked to bring something,—a dessert, a few bags of chips, a six-pack of soda—to help offset costs. Then the hard work began, admits Paula—dividing the guests into four teams and organizing a volleyball game, relay races, pie-eating contests, and other events.

"The day before the Olympics, I began to doubt whether this was such a good idea after all. I worried that despite all my planning and enthusiasm, the whole thing would fall flat on its face. But when 16 excited families arrived wearing T-shirts in their assigned team colors, carrying cakes and platters of hors d'oeuvres, and filled with loads of spirit, I began to relax. They were so grateful for the chance to meet other neighbors with kids the same ages as theirs. And when most asked when Olympics II would be held, I knew we had started a tradition."

how come i feel so disconnected
if this is such a user-friendly world?

102

Not Only Moms Can Run a Playgroup . . .

A Saturday morning playgroup was the brainstorm of Jon, a father in his early 30s, who through his children's nursery school met three other fathers in the neighborhood. All had Saturday morning "babysitting duty" to free up their wives for a few hours.

"So one day I thought, why not hook up like mothers do all the time? We started a weekly playgroup, ten to twelve on Saturday mornings, rotating homes, where the kids could play. When the weather's nice, we meet at a local playground, which is easier since there are ten kids among us. Honestly, I don't think any of us expected to enjoy the time together as much as we do—just hanging out, which most of us never get to do. Our wives are amazed at how organized we are; when it's my turn for playgroup, I even remember to make coffee!"

So might it be with instilling a sense of community within our neighborhoods. By accepting a shared responsibility, by letting our friends and neighbors know that their ideas count and that their strength is needed, we give those we ask a greater meaning to their existence and a deeper purpose to their life.

> **Use your neighbors . . . and encourage them to use you. You don't have to be a good friend to be a good neighbor.**

Location, location, location. It sells real estate, makes or breaks businesses, and turns strangers into neighbors. While most neighbors fall short of the best-friends-forever model illustrated by Lucy and Ethel, Ralph and Norton, and Mary and Rhoda, they are still a principal source of routine companionship and an indispensable aid for minding children and pets.

Unfortunately, many of us don't take advantage of this helpmate right under our noses. We expect too much when we judge our neighbors by the same standards by which we judge our friends. We need our friends for emotional support; we need our neighbors to water our plants.

The expression "Could you do me a favor?" must have been uttered for the first time between two neighbors. Extend yourself to be a good neighbor, and you'll feel a bit more connected to your community. Families with good neighboring relationships are more likely to vote and to believe they have influence with local government. And though relations with neighbors are practical and specialized in nature, they can provide hard-to-come-by peace of mind.

Although many neighboring ties are rather weak, most of us know approximately a dozen neighbors well enough to say hello to on the street.[1] Even if they don't supply the intimacy and warmth of our friendships, they do give us a sense of belonging to a place. It's okay that they won't lend us money or

Why We Need Neighbors

You need contact with your neighbors to ensure that someone will:

- call you if your house is on fire
- let you know if there's a stranger lurking about
- have ketchup, blue thread, antifreeze, or your house key at exactly the right moment
- take in the mail and feed the cat when you're gone
- accept that urgent UPS package that arrives before you get home
- take a picture of your family—you included—on your way to graduation
- run you over to the gas station to pick up your car after it's been serviced
- join you in protesting bad cable TV reception, infrequent garbage pick-ups, or an unreliable corner traffic light
- give Halloween candy that you don't have to check for razor blades

how come i feel so disconnected
if this is such a user-friendly world?

104

listen to our latest fight with the boss; the function they fulfill, utilitarian though it may be, is irreplaceable. The upkeep of neighbor relationships need not be terribly demanding. The nice thing about relationships based on practicality is that it's not even necessary to particularly like a person to depend on them. Just acknowledge that to "use someone" and "be used by someone" (as long as it's mutually beneficial) are not pejorative terms.

Learn the meaning of community spirit. Create your own or join an ongoing neighborhood togetherness project.

According to recent studies by a number of social scientists, the good old days weren't half as good as we think they were. Karen E. Campbell, professor of sociology at Vanderbilt University, analyzed data collected in 1939 from 54 residents of a square block in Bloomington, Indiana. The findings—that the majority of relationships were ones between nodding acquaintances rather than close friends—cast doubts on our assumption that past neighborhood networks were significantly more sociable than contemporary ones. In fact, the "good new days" offer us more opportunities to be creative and stay connected within our community.[2]

Unite for safety–start a neighborhood watch.

Worry—who, us? Why not just sit back, relax, and be happy? In an ideal world, it might work. But reality hums a different tune. Even in neighborhoods that seem safe, statistics tell us otherwise.

Remember the clichés "Better safe than sorry," "There's strength in numbers," and "United we stand, divided we fall"? It's time to take them seriously.

Neighbors who participate in a neighborhood watch must learn how to observe and report suspicious activities to law enforcement agencies and what steps to take to make their homes and neighborhoods less attractive to criminals.

Since the first neighborhood watch program was started in Los Angeles during the late 1960s, more than 19 million Americans have become involved in these programs. Besides reducing crime, active programs bond neighbors and bring a renewed sense of community. Not only is a close-knit, low-crime neighborhood good for our own peace of mind, but it also boosts property values.[3]

Starting a neighborhood watch in your community is easier than you might think. Interested?

"People Helping People" to the Rescue!

"People Helping People" connects developmentally disabled adults in a Long Island community with senior citizens who need help with shopping, gardening, laundry, and housekeeping—tasks that seniors might find too physically stressful. The participating developmentally disabled adults are trained to perform a variety of jobs. The program is an opportunity for them to work for pay outside of a sheltered workshop—giving them confidence and a sense of worth.

Bob Costanzo, executive director of Umbrella, the not-for-profit organization that created "People Helping People," explains that, for many seniors, being able to hire a handyman at affordable rates is a blessing. As Bob explains, "Interdependence leads to independence for both the seniors and the assistants. It's a win-win situation for everyone!" Just ask Blanche, one of the seniors, who admits that her windows hadn't been washed for three years because she couldn't afford it. "The handyman came on the day of my 75th birthday," she remembers. "Sparkling windows was one of the best presents I received!"

how come i feel so disconnected
if this is such a user-friendly world?

106

More Help

If your local law enforcement office doesn't sponsor a neighborhood watch program, two organizations can provide you with information to get your community started:

- The National Sheriffs' Association offers a Neighborhood Watch sample kit for $3.00, including brochures on crime prevention and decals.

    National Sheriffs' Association

    1450 Duke Street

    Alexandria, VA 22314-3490

- The National Crime Prevention Council offers a free crime-prevention information packet, including booklets with crime-prevention tips and sources for additional information.

    National Crime Prevention Council

    Dept. F-1

    1700 K Street NW, 2nd Floor

    Washington, DC 20006-3817

1. Contact your local police department or sheriff's office. If it sponsors a neighborhood watch—and most do—request a date and time that an officer could meet with your group.

2. After the date is set for your first meeting, post fliers around the neighborhood. Include the date, time, and place of the meeting and encourage neighbors to attend.

3. Follow the simple steps recommended by the officer to make homes less inviting to burglars.

4. Make a pact with each of your neighbors to look out for each other.

5. Adopt the attitude of a good citizen: if you observe someone or something suspicious in your neighborhood, immediately call the police.[4]

Make the effort to introduce yourself to the people you deal with at the stores you patronize regularly.

No doubt about it, it's very comforting to shop where everybody knows your name. But how often does this happen anymore? Today we sacrifice the personal touch for the efficiency and ease of buying goods in Texas-size stores stocked with the ultimate assortment of every product known to man and woman. The supermarket's computer might know who you are, but chances are the human operating it won't.

In many communities, except for the rare shoemaker and tailor, there's hardly a retailer who would recognize a familiar face—much less greet a customer by name. What happened to Main Street, filled with the warm neighborhood feeling of mom-and-pop stores—a book store, a pharmacy, a five-and-ten, a bike store, a pet supply store, and a soda shop—where the owners really cared that we came back? Knocked out of business by "Superstores R Us," they're a fast-dying breed. But they're not dead yet.

We can fight the superstores' assault on our sense of community by spending a few more minutes and a few more dollars—and regularly patronizing the small stores around. Those who haven't been eaten up by what economists call "the category killers" will welcome you with open arms. You might not find as complete a selection of goods at the lowest possible price, but you will find a neighborhood businessman who will bend over backwards to please you and mean it when he says, "Have a nice day."

how come i feel so disconnected
if this is such a user-friendly world?

108

A Man with a Mission Makes a Difference

"These superstores were really starting to get to me," says Barry, a frustrated 40-year-old consumer. "Finally, my wife got tired of hearing me complain and challenged me to do something about it. So I did!

"Within a mile of our home is a strip of about ten small stores. I'm embarrassed to admit that except for the candy store, I had never been inside any of them. My mission was cut out for me. That week I started with the hardware store to pick up the light bulbs on my errands list—no more Home Depot! While I was there I made a point of introducing myself to the owner. It felt awkward at first but his friendliness made it easier. Then, on to the deli for a few odd items and the camera store to get our film developed—same routine.

"Beginning with eye contact and a smile, I eased my way in, introducing myself on the second visit. The store owners seemed to appreciate the personal contact. And on my next time in, when each of them greeted me by name, I felt that my business was really important to them."

Invest the time to explore the hidden resources in your community.

Don't throw away that Penny-saver—at least not before you've checked its weekly local calendar of events. Just as single people are advised that the best way to meet someone new is to engage in an interest or activity that brings them pleasure, so, too, is this the best way to connect with your neighborhood. While you're solving a problem, satisfying a curiosity, sharpening a skill, or pursuing a hobby, a likely byproduct might well be a welcome feeling of belonging.

No matter what you're into, we guarantee you'll find others into the same thing if you investigate the following options:

1. The library. Check out the public library's offerings of free movies, lectures, exhibits, and a calendar of upcoming events. Scan the bulletin board and pick up the fliers.

2. The hospital. More and more hospitals are doing community outreach programs that include lectures, discussions, and support groups on various health issues.

3. The book store. Although part of the superstore phenomenon, large book stores are often divided into smaller, more intimate areas. There's comfortable seating where you can enjoy an evening of jazz, a cup of cappuccino, or a book discussion and signing by an invited author.

4. Civic associations. If you want to know what a warm welcome feels like, walk into the closest neighborhood association, environmental study group, school board meeting, or political gathering place.

5. The high school or local community college. Courses in everything from computers to Thai cooking to dream analysis are offered in a relaxed atmosphere at a nominal fee.

6. The community center. The definition of community center goes beyond the gymnasium of days long gone. The Ys of the '90s serve up a variety of family fare, from swimming and photography to parenting workshops and holiday crafts.

7. Clubs. All kinds of clubs are always looking for new members. Read the classified section of your local newspaper and shoppers' guide for information.

Quench your needs for individuality and assimilation–join a peer group.

Who are we, anyway? First we've been told that we are what we eat. (Am I chunky or smooth? Spicy or bland?) Then that we are what we

how come i feel so disconnected
if this is such a user-friendly world?

110

Joining a Group: What's in It for You?

Along with the sense of belonging that comes of being part of a social or interest group are a number of other benefits. When a random sampling of "groupies" were asked why they like being part of a group, here's what they said:

- *"It motivates me," says Randy of her exercise group, which meets at 7 a.m. three days a week. "If I didn't commit to this group, I'd find a million excuses to not exercise consistently. Now I look forward to starting my days moaning and groaning with six other women who are as tired and overscheduled as I am."*

- *"It's a source of discipline," adds Ron about his book group that meets the last Thursday of the month to discuss the work the ten of them have chosen to read. "I love to read, but, between the job and my kids, I never found the time. Being in this group forces me to read— at least one book every month."*

- *"It's inspirational," says Sally, speaking of the local small-business owners group that she started eight years ago. "We began with four members and now have twenty. We meet monthly but network constantly, feeding off one another's ideas for marketing, advertising, and promotions. The shot in the arm our group has given to local business is just a byproduct of our increased self-confidence and pride in our accomplishments."*

do. (If I work from home instead of an office, wear jeans and T-shirts instead of suits, and spend more time with my computer than with other humans—what does that make me?) Now experts are telling us that we're a reflection of the groups we belong to.

Joining a book group doesn't make you a bookworm, and being in an exercise group doesn't mean you're a jock, but who we spend time with is an important ingredient in crafting our self-image. Whether we use a peer group to expand our minds, tone our bodies, improve our businesses, share our secrets, or just pass the time, the benefits convince us how worthwhile it is to join, commit, and share.

It's impossible to truly help someone else without helping yourself as well. Volunteer.

The volunteer spirit in America is thriving. Included in a growing population of American men and women without enough hours in a day are more than 80 million volunteers, of whom 21 million give five or more hours a week to help others.[5]

Concerns that a workforce made up of dual-career families would have a negative impact on volunteerism are easing. Despite our often weary, overworked, overstressed bodies and minds, we are moving beyond the "Me Generation" and toward a sense of community; we are becoming increasingly involved in the plight of people in need.

A national study by University of Virginia sociology professor Steven L. Nock sampled 1,600 people to compare the rate of membership in voluntary organizations between two-earner families and families in which mothers stay at home. Has volunteerism been hurt since more moms are working and nobody's home anymore? Are two-earner couples less likely to volunteer? Quite the contrary, says Dr. Nock, who found that couples who both work are more likely than those with stay-at-home moms to become volunteers—a most encouraging trend.[6]

While researchers were at first surprised at these findings, they soon realized the logic—working couples have more contact with

how come i feel so disconnected
if this is such a user-friendly world?

112

people outside the home and are more likely to be exposed to volunteer opportunities calling for their help. Many dual-career couples have even found that they've reduced the strain of a demanding occupation by taking on another. How? By giving time and thought to a serious concern outside the workplace, they widen their world in a positive way. When your time, energy, and creativity are needed to plan the annual fund-raiser for Cancer Care, you have no choice but to stop worrying about the sales, profits, and projections of your own business—at least for a little while.

"What is a house but a bigger skin, and a neighborhood map but the world's skin ever expanding?"

—Annie Dillard

Furthermore, volunteerism is increasing dramatically among young people. More than 60 percent of the students at the University of Virginia are involved in some form of outreach program or volunteer activity. This spirit is flourishing on college campuses across America, says Al Splete, president of the Council of Independent Colleges.

In 1993 the Council received a $1.5 million grant to implement a service learning project known as Learning to Serve/Serving to Learn. Its goal is to solidify the volunteer effort among students. "We're trying to expand the curriculum on college campuses, to include good-will activities and instill a spirit of giving something of yourself to improve the world," says Al. "We're teaching students today that part of being a responsible citizen is looking out for your neighbor. If we can get kids to start early, our hope is that this volunteer spirit will be lasting."[7]

If volunteering feels good, do it! Research from a national survey reported by Alan Luks and Peggy Payne in *The Healing Power of Doing Good* showed that:

- Ninety-five percent of volunteers get a "helper's high"—a physical feel-good sensation—from helping on a regular basis.

- Nine out of 10 experience sudden warmth and increased energy or a sense of euphoria.

- Volunteers who report these sensations view their health as better than that of others their age.

- Those who are most likely to experience the feel-good sensation are those who have personal contact with the people they help.

And if that isn't enough, volunteers report gaining benefits that they never imagined when they first signed up. Among them:

- New skills. Often unexpected ones, like learning karate from emotionally disturbed kids at a special school. Or learning computer skills while volunteering at Planned Parenthood. From public speaking to cooking to plain "people" skills like listening and making new friends, the opportunities are abundant.

Making a Difference

"Can you spare one hour a week to help stamp out illiteracy? Help someone learn to read. Make a friend. Make a difference."

The poster on the bulletin board of her local supermarket haunted Marci's conscience for weeks before she finally succumbed and called the local office of Literacy Volunteers of America. The following Tuesday, after an interview and training session, Marci met Rosita, and she officially became a volunteer tutor. "The revelation hit me like a ton of bricks," admits Marci. "Sure, I'm busy. I work full time and have two kids to take care of. Everyone I know is busy. But if we all kept that 'this is meant for the other guy but not for me' attitude, nobody would ever reach out to help anybody else."

how come i feel so disconnected
if this is such a user-friendly world?

114

Finding Your Niche

"When I retired, I wanted to do something but didn't know what," explains Phil. "What can a retired accountant do? Then I heard of an agency that provides assistance in income tax preparation and financial planning for people who can't afford to pay for the services. I could do what I had been doing for forty years—to an incredibly appreciative audience. I had found my calling."

- New friends. While friendship is not the motivating factor of most who volunteer, many lasting relationships are formed among fellow volunteers. At Susquehanna College, where theme cottages have become a growing trend, students who volunteer together found that they have so much in common that they are grouping together to live.

- Career benefits. Of course we don't volunteer in order to advance our career, but the people we meet along the way might one day be viable contacts who will remember our unselfishness and reward us with a reference, job lead, or favor.

- New outlooks and personal insight. Volunteer jobs are unpaid, but the perks are there. No matter where we unselfishly turn our attention, we are enriched by the experience. Along with a greater appreciation of our own average, boring days, we increase our repertoire of skills, add to our contacts, and broaden our perspectives. Making a positive difference in the lives of others empowers and endears us in ways no other activity can.[8]

Choose a volunteer experience that's suited for you. In some families volunteerism is inherited. If your grandfather was a volunteer fireman, odds are your father followed in his footsteps and you too will be (or already are) sitting around the local firehouse waiting to serve your community. If a relative suffers from cystic fibrosis or muscular dystrophy or is a victim of leukemia, a drunk-driving accident, or Alzheimer's disease, chances are great that your volunteer efforts will be directed toward a related cause. But for those of us with no volunteer legacy, choosing a volunteer opportunity is a more conscious process.

If you're a voracious reader, a gourmet cook, or a good listener, there are volunteer opportunities calling your name. Ever think about reading books onto tapes for the blind? Giving cooking lessons to disabled adults? Working on a crisis hotline? No skills ever need be wasted.

There is certainly no shortage of opportunities—anyone with a good heart

So You'd Like to Volunteer?

Here's a guide, provided by The United Way of Long Island, to help you choose a volunteer opportunity. Consider:

1. Your skills and interests
   - Why do you want to volunteer? Will the volunteer position you choose fulfill your volunteer goals?
   - Do you have any special interests, hobbies, or talents that you would like to use in a volunteer activity?
   - Would you like to give technical assistance to an organization, join a committee, be an adviser—even serve on the board of directors?
2. Your available time
   - How many hours a week or a month would you like to volunteer?
   - How long-range a commitment are you willing to make?
3. The setting you prefer
   - In what kind of an organization do you want to work—hospital, day-care center, school, senior center, office?
   - With whom do you want to work—children, the elderly, the disabled, the homeless?
   - Do you want to work in a fast-paced or quiet environment?
4. Personal considerations
   - Do you have access to transportation? Is public transportation available? Is there parking?
   - Do you have any physical or emotional difficulties which should be considered when selecting a volunteer job?

how come i feel so disconnected
if this is such a user-friendly world?

116

Reality Check–We're Listening

Conservatively estimated, 15 million Americans attend about 50,000 support group meetings each week. Whether seeking information and resources to ease a business crisis or recovering from addictive behavior, sharing tips and encouragement to overcome cancer or dealing with discrimination— people welcome the healing power these groups provide. The number of people experiencing the benefits of such programs has more than quadrupled since 1980.[9]

can become a volunteer in a matter of minutes. In most towns and cities there are volunteer coordinating organizations—volunteers who help volunteers to find a place to volunteer. Don't hesitate to get help in matching your skills, talents, and interests to the specific needs of an organization.

And remember: you're in demand; the choice is yours. The better suited you are for the volunteer job you choose, the more effective you'll be.

In the raging river, grab onto the branch otherwise known as a support group.

If your family is too far away, your friends are too busy to listen, and you're missing an outlet that's safe, nonjudgmental, and empowering, a support group might fill the gap.

Fewer of us nowadays are burdened with the notion that smart and successful people handle everything that comes along without advice. Asking for help, especially from those who've "been there," is less a sign of inadequacy than a badge of emotional honesty. With Freud came the understanding that our feelings and emotions can be improved through communication. And with the proliferation of thousands of mutual help groups comes the comfort that acknowledging our limitations and increasing our interdependence makes us stronger.

Support groups infuse us with a sense of community. They work so well because their structure allows us the flexibility we need. Anyone can join or form one anytime, anywhere, for any purpose. Move, and latch on to another local branch. Meetings are "power-free" zones, where the focus is on awareness of the bond that brings everyone together, not the individuals in the group. We search out people to talk to whom we won't see every day or run into at social activities.

Support groups don't demand a lot of time, just our trust and confidentiality. They grow and change in response to the group's needs and pressures, and when they are no longer useful, they disband. We can reveal as much or as little as feels comfortable—as long as we tell the truth. And whether our goal is problem oriented or growth oriented, we can find the confidence to achieve it by depending not on a powerful leader or expert but on our peers.

Starting Your Own Support Group: A Success Story

Joy started her own support group for former career women like herself who decided to stay home to care for their children. She solicited participants by putting notices on the bulletin boards of four nursery schools near her home.

"I got nine calls," says Joy. "Seven women showed up to the first meeting, and six remained for the group's eighteen-month lifetime. Two of the women were friends; the rest of us had familiar faces and similar resumes. The format that worked best for us was to come up with a question at the end of each meeting to be discussed the following week. We talked about how we felt about not having 'our own' money, when was the right time to go back to work, how to handle babysitters and mothers-in-law and former colleagues who really didn't understand why you're not back at work. It was wonderful. We shared favorite books, vacation tips, and thoughtful, honest feedback. We goaded each other to investigate intriguing job opportunities and take computer courses to update our skills."

how come i feel so disconnected
if this is such a user-friendly world?

118

To find like minds, whether your issues are centered around the family, health, career, avocation, or politics, check out your newspaper's classified ads, community bulletin boards, the library, or your local self-help clearinghouse.

Get an attitude adjustment. It is never too late to give up your prejudices.

Many of us grew up in ethnically homogeneous cultures where we recognized, in faces that looked like ours, a kinship. Even if our community wasn't a small town, we generally knew everyone else's business because it wasn't remarkably different from our own. Even if we were raised to "look out for number one," we still empathized with our neighbors and felt sympathy, compassion, sorrow, and pity if their experiences called for it.

Those of us who haven't altered our definition of neighborhood since those days are having a tough time. Some of our neighbors might no longer look, speak, and dress the same way we do. Because we're uncomfortable with what's not familiar, we become stingy with our empathy and close ourselves off to the wonder and spiciness that accompanies diversity. We could handle the multiculturalism in our community more easily if our new neighbors were more eager to assimilate. The metaphor of America as a "melting pot" no longer applies; nationalities that once strove to "melt" into the woodwork now try to maintain their identity and cultivate their special origins.

Our fear of what we don't know extends beyond our foreign neighbors. NIMBYism (Not-In-My-Back-Yard-ism) has interfered with the forward progress of communities all over the country. Group homes for handicapped adults, drug treatment centers, shelters for the homeless, and outpatient psychiatric clinics have been voted down (in sad examples of communal togetherness) hundreds of times. Too often today we are more passionately linked to our neighbors by the unpredictable and frightening than by the comfort of friendship. Wouldn't it be wonderful if a more generous inclusivity became our communal rallying point in the 1990s?

Doing the right thing in this case might not come naturally. Take a risk and open yourself up to new opportunities. Smile first. Make eye contact and wave hello. Former U.S. Representative Barbara Jordan had some good advice: "If everybody you invite into your life for a drink or dinner all look just like you, why not invite a friend from a different race or ethnic group to come to your house? If we could expand the horizon of people we respect, it would take us a long way toward ending racism. You cannot dislike, distrust, or hate people you respect."

"I'd Like to Welcome My New Neighbors, But . . . "

Judy, who lives in a suburb of New York that has seen a large influx of Korean, Chinese, Indian, and Persian families over the last five years, is struggling with this issue. "Asian families now live in three of the ten houses that surround mine," she explains. "I grew up defining a neighbor as someone you shared leftover birthday cake with and held an extra key for in case they lost theirs. I am embarrassed to admit I never even introduced myself to these families. I guiltily wonder, if the situation were reversed and I moved to where they came from, whether they would be more hospitable. But the language barrier, the fact that we never run into one another, and a hectic working-mother style of life puts being a warm welcoming neighbor on my permanent wish list."

how come i feel so disconnected
if this is such a user-friendly world?

120

• CLOSING THOUGHTS

Often many of us have felt that, as individuals, we can't do much to make a difference in this world. Self-negatingly we say, "What change can my few dollars (my three hours) possibly make? Who'll notice whether or not I show up for a neighborhood clean-up meeting? Will it really matter if I join . . . belong . . . attend?"

There's a true story told of Sir Michael Costa, a renowned symphony conductor of a generation or two ago. During the playing of a symphony, at a moment when the hall was filled by the thunder of the mighty organ and the great roll of the massive drums, at the peak of climactic crescendo, the piccolo player said to himself, "With so much volume, my insignificant instrument doesn't really matter." So he stopped playing.

Suddenly, the maestro signaled; the orchestra and the music came to an abrupt halt. The sudden quiet of that moment was dramatically broken by Costa shouting, "Where is the piccolo?"

No one of us is, in the world of reality, so small or so insignificant that our sound is not heard or our silence not lamented. Our lives have a specific and vital part to play and a difference to make in the complex design of events that is life's symphony.

For a different spin on a similar melody, the Business Partnership for Peace offers its motto:

If you think you can't change the world by yourself, join some people who agree.

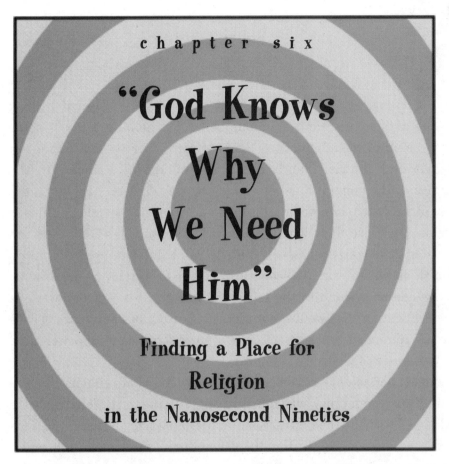

chapter six

"God Knows Why We Need Him"

Finding a Place for Religion in the Nanosecond Nineties

"But what is religion? I for one would answer: Not the religion you would get after reading all the Scriptures of the world. Religion is not what is grasped by the brain, but a heart grasp."
—Mahatma Gandhi

how come i feel so disconnected
if this is such a user-friendly world?

122

No matter how superficial and transient our lives might look on the outside, a serious religious belief can help protect our souls from being bent and spindled. As we listen, over the mutterings of Beavis and Butthead and the clamor of Mortal Kombat, to the stories of the generations before us, we may find an age-old choice less difficult to make: today it might just be easier to believe than to doubt. On those days when the world is too much with us—when sinister little voices whisper, "Who do you think you are?" "What do you think you're worth?"—coming together to worship is invaluable. As we glance around to the left and the right, we are comforted in the realization that we are not alone in our doubts and fears. There we are reminded that each of us is a most significant being, created in the image of God.

A most persistent—and misleading—myth is that religion, like the family and community, was much stronger in the past. That "old time religion," without the distractions and temptations of today, was actually no more pious. In nineteenth-century America, church membership as a proportion of the total population was only about half of what it is now, and attendance was probably no better. Recent Gallup polls have found that nine out of ten Americans claim to believe in God; 60 percent affirm the importance of prayer in their lives, and 85 percent say that religion is "very" or "fairly" important to them.[1]

Today we are not as concerned with what's handed down from the Vatican or Jerusalem or Salt Lake City as we are with what's served up in our own local house of worship. While we find the traditional chants and liturgy comforting, our presence is more about belonging to a family than about subscribing to a creed. The sermons we are listening to with most interest deal not with how to be more perfectly devout but with how to be more openly human.

The issues that trouble us—What do we have after we have everything? What do we matter? What does life mean?—are being addressed by a more flexible, more accessible clergy. Our observance is less a matter of obeying or pleasing God than a matter of committing to bettering ourselves and the world around us.

> *"All human beings have an intimate need to hear and tell stories and to have a story to live by . . . religion, whatever else it has done, has provided one of the main ways of meeting this abiding need."*
> *—Harley Cox*

Religion, '90s style, is moving beyond the script, beyond texts and rhetoric and entrenched authority. Rituals are valuable as long as their meaning can be transmitted into the essence of our lives. Many of us who are attending services on a more regular and sustained basis are doing so not because we're fearful or guilty, but because the spiritual strength our faith offers better enables us to face the day's uncertainties.

Most of us are familiar with the words of Robert Frost:

> *The woods are lovely, dark and deep.*
> *But I have promises to keep,*
> *And miles to go before I sleep.*

how come i feel so disconnected
if this is such a user-friendly world?

124

You may not know that later, when he was asked what promises he had in mind, Frost replied: "Oh, promises to myself and promises to my ancestors."

Each of us makes such promises to ourselves. Most of the time they are phrased in words or written out over our signatures. But sometimes they are expressed in the silent sanctuary of our own soul: to surrender a destructive habit, to abandon some self-defeating behavior, to effect reconciliation with a relative or friend, to show more affection to a mate and more attention to a child, to give more time to matters of the spirit.

Simplistic values of self-righteousness will no longer work to entice future generations to grab hold of their religious heritage and traditions. Our task is to make our religious experiences meaningful by connecting them to broader patterns of thinking and behaving. And we must do so in the midst of the most mobile and individualistic society ever on earth.

As daunting as the job might be, its rewards make the effort worthwhile. As with physical exercise, it might take awhile before we realize significant benefits from a return to a more spiritual life. Our streets are frequented by joggers who will never run a marathon; local tennis courts are filled with players who will never make it to the U.S. Open. But all are striving to make progress, to become a little better, a little healthier. We can do exactly the same thing in our moral and spiritual lives. We can each expand our heart capacity, at least a little. And if our kids emulate our behavior, if our children get "it"—the real experience of spiritual connectedness—they'll be back for support and renewal for the rest of their lives.

Respect the power of prayer. The way we talk to God is the best barometer of our religious commitment.

We can pray when we're relaxed and listening to music; while we're on line, vacuuming, or commuting; as we fall asleep; or when we're panicked and can't do anything but. If you want more options, there are over 2,000 books on prayer meditation and techniques for spiritual growth—three times more than on sexual intimacy.[2]

You might find it hard to believe, but in self-centered, aerobic-intensive America, more people (78 percent!) will pray this week than exercise or have sex.[3] We're nervous talking about it—what we say, when we do it, and how we feel about it. Prayer is probably the only subject so private it's never been discussed on Oprah.

Almost two decades ago, Sir Alister Hardy, a biologist at Oxford University, decided that science had lost sight of the spiritual aspects of life. So he compiled over 5,000 accounts of adults who had admitted having religious experiences, ranging from miraculous healings to feelings of unusual harmony with the universe. He found that one in every three Britons had had such an experience. But he also found that most had chosen to keep quiet about it for fear of being thought stupid—or worse yet, religious!

It gets sticky talking about our souls—the place where we diverge from the animals, where we fall in love, where we experience awe and hope and faith. Prayer is a complex, multifaceted phenomenon

> *"Now and again, in the synagogue or the woods, in the bedroom or the nursery, in the concert hall or the theatre, we are visited by a moment of transcendence; but we do not suppose that we might live there, the air is too thin at the peak and besides, there's bread to be earned and the Superbowl is on this afternoon."*
>
> —Leonard Fein

how come i feel so disconnected
if this is such a user-friendly world?

126

> *"I have never met a healthy person who worries very much about his health or a really good person who worries much about his own soul."*
>
> —J. B. S. Haldane

that rewards us with a sense of believing and belonging. Prayer reflects the outcome of our personal relationships with other people and, unlike the rest of life, is most successful when we allow ourselves to let down our guard.

Many of us walk around with a very narrow notion of what prayer entails. Canned prayer, whether it is practiced with discipline by the rules at a certain time and place or involves petitioning a supergenie for favors, is not what we're talking about here. Rather than granting miracles by thunderbolt, the God we're relating to centers us, calms us, and offers strength. The solitude of prayer demands we face ourselves without the pretense that aids us in bluffing our way through the day.

Waiting for enough faith to pray is like waiting for inspiration to write . . . pointless. We need to carve an eye of peace out of the hurricane of our days and let the tension drain. More important than any "promises to keep" is grabbing the opportunity to reflect on what is really important in our lives. We have to trust that this is one arena where there's no right and wrong and, in the language of silence, focus on letting go and letting ourselves be.

Take a few deep breaths, slow down, turn inward, and discover the restorative ability of prayer.

There's not only one way or time or place to pray. Like Goldilocks, we have to try a lot of things to find which "feels" best. Some find prayer best on rising in the morning; others pray after the supper dishes are done, after the late news, or once in bed, right before sleep. Some like to sit quietly; others prefer walking; still others pretzel themselves into a lotus. But the most important element is to have a focus to come back to when you're distracted. And you will be distracted. Your stomach gurgles; your legs cramp; your nose itches as you suddenly remember, "I didn't return that library book!" The focus brings you back to your center.

Dr. Herbert Benson, professor of medicine at Harvard Medical School and author of *The Relaxation Response,* says that the words may vary, but the benefits don't. So far Dr. Benson has trained scores of ministers, rabbis, priests, and nuns to achieve the relaxation response through prayer. He teaches a very simple way to achieve the relaxation response, using one's own belief system.

Choose a word or a short phrase from your religion. Repeat the word or phrase silently to yourself, coordinating it with your

The Chosen Word

For a focus word or phrase related to your own religious tradition, Dr. Benson recommends the following:

- For Roman Catholics and Christians with similar traditions: The Jesus Prayer ("Lord Jesus Christ, have mercy on me"), an excerpt from the Lord's Prayer ("Our Father who art in heaven"), a line from the Hail Mary ("Hail Mary, full of grace"), or a line from the Apostles' Creed ("I believe in the Holy Spirit").
- For Protestants: Words from Psalm 23 ("The Lord is my shepherd") or from Psalm 100 ("Make a joyful noise unto the Lord"); any of Jesus' teachings or words, such as "My peace I give unto you" (John 14:27), "Love one another" (John 15:12), or "I am the way, the truth, and the life" (John 14:6).
- For Jews: The Hebrew words for peace (*shalom*), One (*Echod*), or the Name (*Ha-Shem*); any passage from the Hebrew Bible, such as "Thou shalt love thy neighbor" (Leviticus 19:8).[4]

how come i feel so disconnected
if this is such a user-friendly world?

128

breathing if that's most comfortable. The words should be easy to pronounce and to remember, and short enough to say silently as you exhale. When thoughts arise, as they inevitably will, gently return to the focus word or phrase. You'll begin enjoying periods of stillness and quiet in your mind. Ideally, this practice should be done for at least 10 minutes a day.

Revive your commitment to your church or temple.

There's a reason no primitive society without a religion has ever been found. Whether you need a bandage for a battered soul, an injection of humility, a reminder of the worth of "give" over "take," or a quiet place to recall the rituals and habits of your childhood, the doors of your local place of worship are open and welcoming. Even if you've never been part of a congregation before, enter and meet the family.

In a typical church on a typical Sunday, the congregation is slightly older than the population as a whole. According to recent polls, they are healthier and much more likely to say that they are happy and satisfied with their lives than their neighbors who are sleeping in or reading the papers over a leisurely breakfast. Why? And how do we get over the obstacles that make joining them so difficult?[5]

According to a study conducted by Wade Clark Roof, professor of religion and society at the University of California at Santa Barbara, two thirds of the generation born from 1946 to 1962 stopped active religious observance when they left their parents' homes. Of those, about 40 percent eventually returned to some contact with their religious institution—and many more are considering renewing their affiliation.[6]

Congregations were traditionally built around small communities where people lived, worked, and worshipped together. Life-jolting events—birth, death, serious health problems, accidents, violence—were shared by neighbors and friendly acquaintances. There was a comfort in the familiar hymns, prayers, and chants, a sense of harmony and camaraderie engendered when everyone turned to a force greater than their own egos. A sense of caring, based not on possessions or professional accomplishments but on an unspoken communal bond, healed and strengthened them.

Never more than today have we needed a refuge from our intensely competitive world. Increasingly, there is acknowledgment

Shopping Around for a Moral Compass

"I would have gone on blissfully nonobservant if I hadn't had a child," admits Sherry, mother of an 18-month-old baby. *"I'm afraid that, without the moral safety net of organized religion to reinforce what we teach at home, we'll all be in trouble. Who besides us is our daughter going to get her moral convictions from, her ethical training—if not from the temple? I want to expose her to this touchstone so she can see people doing things for the elderly, the sick, the homeless, and the lonely."*

"I remember a story my grandfather told me," adds Richard, Sherry's husband. *"It's about a group of rabbis who gathered on a special day to light a fire and pray at a certain place in the forest. While these were very learned men, they never taught their skills to the next generation. Eventually those who came only knew how to light the fire, not to say the prayers. And soon there was no one who could even remember the place. All that remained was the story; the rituals that had been performed were lost forever. I know that a lot of my friends today feel the same way. We might have to shop around awhile but I'm confident that we'll find a place that will answer our needs."*

how come i feel so disconnected
if this is such a user-friendly world?

130

of our own frailty and our desire to look beyond ourselves for guidance and sustenance. A serene space far removed from racing pulses awaits. So does the camaraderie of others on the same quest to add spiritual meaning to their lives. God knows, what do you have to lose by trying?

All of us have an innate hunger to hear and tell tales and have a story to live by. For centuries, religion has provided one of the main ways of meeting this need. Now its themes of faith, hope, and charity compete with the 55 channels on our TVs, the millions of commuters on the information highway, and a workweek that allows few hours for quiet respite. For many, devotion and spiritual belief lie dormant, perhaps right next to courage and patience.

But these qualities can be renewed by allowing ourselves to become vulnerable to the cadences, physical setting, and transcendent connecting experiences available at our local church or temple. Like riding a bike, the ability to find solace in a place of worship can return relatively easily after a long absence.

Instill in your children a sense of spirituality.

All kids wonder about the same questions we did when we were their age: Is there a God? What does God look like? Does God talk to people? When I talk to God, does He listen? If God is so good, why is there so much bad in the world?

Answering questions about God is not like answering questions about pizza, write co-authors Rabbi Marc Gellman and Monsignor Thomas Hartman, in *Where Does God Live?*

With a pizza, you've got your basic crust, and your basic tomato sauce, and your basic cheese and your basic toppings and . . . that's a pizza. The reason we know so much about pizzas is that we see pizzas, and eat pizzas, all the time. But God is different from a pizza. God is not like anything else in the world. God cannot be seen and God cannot be smelled. But God is as real as pizza—more real because (although you may find this hard to believe) there was a time before pizza, but there never was a time before God.

Use your church or synagogue for reinforcement. By providing our children with religious education and encouraging them to use their church or synagogue as a social and support base, we are reinforcing the message from home. Sometimes we are warmed by the comfort and familiarity of worshipping at the same church or synagogue that our parents joined years ago. But tradition alone doesn't always make it an automatic fit.

The challenge of the '90s is connecting with a house of worship that our children will go to because they want to, not because they have to. Religious leaders who are dynamic, creative, and open to new ideas are likely to support religious schools and youth groups that reflect their attitudes. For parents, an interview with a rabbi, priest, or minister to talk "philosophy" could be an investment worth far more than the hour it takes. If we belong to a religious institution that is an extension of our own philosophy and attitudes, we have a better chance of relaying our own enthusiasm to the next generation.

• DISCOVERING GOD

The following are some suggestions for books you might find helpful in your own journey:

how come i feel so disconnected
if this is such a user-friendly world?

132

- *Finding God,* by Dr. Larry Crabb (Grand Rapids, Michigan: Zondervan, 1993). Written in an intensely personal style, this book cuts through all the familiar preoccupation with our problems in feeling closer to God. Dr. Crabb's passion and enthusiasm are contagious.

- *How to Think About God: A Guide for the 20th Century Pagan,* by Mortimer J. Adler (New York: Macmillan, 1980). For those who are curious but not convinced about the question of God's existence, this book will give your mind a workout. The author examines and refutes several traditional arguments and comes up with his own theory!

- *I and Thou,* by Martin Buber (Walter Kaufman, trans.; New York: Scribner, 1970). This challenging, original work investigates the possibilities of a direct or immediate relationship with God. The book is difficult, but worth the effort.

- *The Mind of God,* by Paul Davies (New York: Simon & Schuster, 1992). For those more comfortable with a book subtitled "The Scientific Basis for a Rational World," one of England's leading theoreticians uses science as a means of seeing into the mind of God.

- *Looking for God to Pray To: Christian Spirituality in Transition,* by William Reiser (Mahwah, New Jersey: Paulist Press, 1994). The author addresses the conflicts that arise (and how to handle them) when "being a believer" feels like you're playing a game in which the rules (the world, the church, the people around you) have changed without warning.

- *God's Paintbrush,* by Sandy Eisenberg Sasso (Woodstock, Vermont: Jewish Lights, 1992). This sophisticated yet totally accessible book is guaranteed to spark many ongoing discussions about God. It presents a metaphor, then asks a question directly in the text. God is explored through emotions, actions, and His connections to everyday life.

• *Old Turtle,* by Douglas Wood (Duluth: Pfeifer-Hamilton, 1992). This is a beautifully illustrated, charmingly told fable about learning to see God in each other. It's wonderful for all ages, especially teens and adults.

• *Where Does God Live? Questions and Answers for Parents and Children,* by Marc Gellman and Thomas Hartman (New York: Ballantine, 1991). This book's warm, usable question-and-answer format has a twist: its authors are a rabbi and a monsignor. The questions and answers are straightforward and told with a lively sense of humor.

God Talk with Your Children

Gellman and Hartman offer the following guidelines:

• Let your children watch you do the religious things you do. The best way to explain God to children is without words. Letting them see you engaged in religious behavior will do more than a thousand books to stimulate questions and teach them that God is real in your life.

• Tell your children what you believe, while making it clear to them that they must decide for themselves what to believe.

• Don't be afraid to say "I don't know." Follow statements about what you don't "know" with ones about what you "believe."

• Try to relate God to how we live, not just to what we believe. The connection between God and our moral lives must be clear and strong to children.

• Don't give answers about God that are too simple. Children deserve the right to chew on complicated ideas. If you don't believe in God, you can still talk meaningfully to your children about God—explaining that even though you may have doubts about whether God is real, God is still a living force in many people's lives.[7]

how come i feel so disconnected
if this is such a user-friendly world?

134

- *I Learn About God,* by Howard I. Bogot and Daniel B. Syme (New York: UAHC Press, 1982). Specially designed for young readers and preschool children, this book demonstrates that many of the everyday things we do (such as helping a friend, seeing a butterfly come out of its cocoon, or trying our best) can actually be ways of learning about God.

- *God Is a Good Friend to Have,* compiled by Eric Marshall and Stuart Hample (New York: Simon & Schuster, 1969). An "out-of-the-mouths-of-babes" collection of answers to questions like: Who is God? Where do you find Him? How do you know there is a God? What do you know about Him? Guaranteed to make you smile . . . and to reenergize your thinking.

Teach your children about the rewards and pleasures of their heritage.

How can we give our kids a sense of the past while adding richer meaning to their present? When the authors of this book asked this question of parents during our many interviews, we found several recurring themes. Here are some of the ways parents can help children connect with their roots:

Enjoy ongoing rituals together. The specific activity is not as important as the process of sharing. Whether they are daily, weekly, or yearly observances, rituals provide a sense of continuity, constancy, and closeness between parents and children.

Celebrate religious holidays together. Every faith has its own set of holidays, customs, and ceremonies—each associated with at least one legend or tale that explains why we celebrate or do what we do. Most holidays include a unique package of special foods, songs, and ceremonies. The more hands-on (and age-appropriate) activities we do with our children—baking poppy seed cookies at Purim, lighting the candles on the Advent wreath before Christmas, coloring and searching for Easter eggs, singing holiday songs, playing holiday games—the richer these times will be and the more likely that they will remain a lasting part of our children's hearts and souls.

Teach by doing. The spoken message is rarely as effective as that set by example. When we demonstrate ourselves—practice with our children what we want them to "get"—we instill in them the ultimate lesson: "Don't do as I say, but do as I do."

Include kids in a search of family roots. Sharing with our children what we

Family Rituals: Sharing a Sense of Who We Are

For Tom and Kathy, saying prayers with their children before meals brings a sense of peacefulness and harmony. "During the days, we're all off in different directions, often rushed and busier than we'd like," says Tom. "But taking a moment out before dinner to slow down and say our prayers allows us to feel the essence of who we really are."

For David and Robin, lighting the Sabbath candles on Friday nights with their three children creates a feeling of being united with Jews all over the world who are doing the same thing at the same time at the end of the week. "It's a small ritual, but it has amazing power," admits Robin. "First I light the candles and the kids drop a few coins in our tzedakeh, which is a charity box. Then David says a blessing in Hebrew, praying to God that the children will grow strong, healthy, and wise. There's a sense of community and spirituality during this time that for us is what Judaism is all about."

how come i feel so disconnected
if this is such a user-friendly world?

136

discover of our heritage tightens the bonds within the here and now and, at the same time, strengthens their spiritual connections. Of course a family genealogy study won't—and shouldn't—be as exhaustive as one you attempt yourself. But inviting children to make a modified family tree or to come along on an interview to listen to stories about coming to America in 1900 and what kinds of games were played at the turn of the century can have a positive bonding effect.

Visit places that have spiritual meaning. Such places don't have to be churches or synagogues. There are other ways and places to find a spiritual connection. Growing numbers of travelers are taking religious pilgrimages, journeying for miles to seek spiritual experiences and renewal. Lourdes, Europe's most popular Roman Catholic shrine, had more pilgrimages in 1992 than in any year since the apparition of the Virgin Mary was reported there in 1858. The small town in the French Pyrenees had a record 5.5 million visitors. Israel has also become a

It's More Than Just the Challah

"It's hard to put into words what it means to me to be a Jew," explains Elaine. "The most important lesson my kids have gotten over the years has come from watching me prepare for the Sabbath—setting the dining room table with our good china, wine glasses, and candles. We often have guests on Fridays—relatives, friends, sometimes Jewish strangers who are visiting from out of town and contact our synagogue to find out where they might share a Shabbat dinner. We all welcome the constancy: eating challah, drinking wine, catching up on the week as a family. Now that our kids are teenagers, they usually want to go out after dinner on Friday nights. But hopefully they leave with a better sense of who they are and where they come from."

popular tourist attraction for Jews—and non-Jews—from all over the world. A religious revival, laced with shared nostalgia for a less confusing past, might be the motivation.[8]

Give your children names that add meaning to their heritage.

"What's in a name?" asked William Shakespeare in *Romeo and Juliet*. What's in that combination of letters we hear dozens of times every day, that we scribble on checks and memos and write on letters and reports? Is it nothing more than a label of convenience?

Our names are, in fact, an essential part of who we are. Some cultures believe that names are a reflection of their bearers' traits or destiny—that a well-chosen name can bring prosperity, popularity, or power; ward off evil spirits; or chart a successful path for life.

Guidelines for Family Interviews

If your kids are interested in conducting their own genealogical study, offer them a few helpful tips:

1. Before the interview, suggest that they jot down several questions and practice asking them a few times.

2. Ask relatives in advance to gather old family pictures or documents like passports, citizenship papers, marriage certificates, and maps that they can examine with you. This will help them remember stories.

3. Conduct the interview in a quiet place that is comfortable to the interviewee.

4. Suggest some memory-triggering questions: What are your earliest childhood memories? What did you do with your time when you were younger? Did you go to school or work? What was your home like? What do you think was the most important thing that ever happened in your life? What experiences were great adventures to you? What was the biggest decision you ever made?

5. Remind your children that everyone has a story to tell—if only someone would listen; if only someone would ask.

how come i feel so disconnected
if this is such a user-friendly world?

138

Reality Check-Did You Know . . .

1. On a total scale of religiosity—which included measures of weekly church attendance, belief in a personal God, importance of God in one's life, belief in life after death, and obtaining comfort from religion—Americans rated 67 (out of 100), compared to, for example, 36 for Great Britain and 32 for France. Only the Republic of Ireland, with a score of 73, ranked higher than the U.S.[9]

2. Eighty-seven percent of Americans, or about 150 million, claim to be Christian; 1.8 percent, or about 3.1 million, say they are Jewish; about 500,000, or 0.5 percent, say they are Muslim; about 1.2 million say they are agnostic; and about 13 million claim "no religion."[10]

3. Both churchgoing and nonchurchgoing baby boomers, born between 1947 and 1956, are nearly unanimous on the desirability of religious instruction for their children. Earlier involvement in counterculture activities—such as marijuana smoking or involvement in the civil rights, antiwar, or women's liberation movements—has little correlation with whether or not baby boomers are churchgoers as adults.[11]

4. Females attend church far more than males. Women seem more inclined than men to harbor an interest in religion.[12]

5. As reported by a 1990 Associated Press poll, respondents ranked relative importance of various concerns, with the following results: 40 percent said faith in God was the most important thing in their lives; 29 percent said good health was number one; a happy marriage was the choice of 21 percent. Only 2 percent cited a job that pays well.[13]

Since the coming of Christianity, the most popular forenames in western societies have been those of saints or biblical figures. Catholics receive their saint's name at baptism and often a second saint's name at confirmation. Jewish families looked to Old Testament Hebrew forenames as a badge of identity. Puritans added names that reflected virtues they esteemed and hoped to transmit to their children: Prudence, Constance, and Charity for girls; Increase, Preserved, and Learned for boys. While the more extreme Puritan names went out of fashion, religious tradition in name selection remains strong in western culture.

The 20th century has brought with it a name explosion. Out went John and Mary; in came Jason and Jennifer. Out went ordinary; in came novelty, originality, and individuality—names with an image. But even after three centuries of sweeping changes, standard English and biblical names still dominate. A revival of traditional names such as Sara, Jane, Emma, and Max; a growing return to biblical names such as Joshua, Leah, and Hannah; and, among African Americans, use of such names as Keisha, Jamal, Tonica, and Delonte are evidence that growing numbers of new parents are looking to feel a connection with their heritage and resurrect ancestral ties.[14]

No More Sermons–Now There Are Roundtable Discussions

Is changing religious architecture a reflection of a new attitude?

No question about it, says Rabbi Arthur Schwartz, of Kehillath Shalom in Cold Spring Harbor, New York. On any given day congregants may find their seats placed in sections to face each other or perhaps arranged in a circle. The seating arrangements always change to keep from getting stale and to promote an active, people-centered congregation, explains Rabbi Schwartz. Instead of a service station where people pop in and out to get a bar mitzvah, the synagogue is a continuous support network.

"What would you be willing to do for another congregant?" new members are asked when they join the synagogue. "Are you a first-hand expert on breast cancer? Prostate cancer? Can you drive? Cook? Babysit?" When a fellow congregant is having a personal crisis, he or she can call the synagogue and immediately be put in touch with an appropriate support. Rabbi Schwartz explains, "For a woman told by her doctor that she has breast cancer, the comfort of having another woman who's already been through it show up at her front door within an hour, hold her hand, and talk her through the crisis is what the spirit of the synagogue has become all about."

how come i feel so disconnected
if this is such a user-friendly world?

140

"Doubt is part of all religion. All the religious thinkers were doubters."
—Isaac Bashevis Singer

Parents today may be more adventurous and creative in using variations or unusual spellings of the original name, or in giving their children American equivalents for traditional biblical names, or in giving their children both a middle name with significance and a first name for the '90s. But the spirit of connection is there. Our names are our identities—and your family heritage should be one of your children's proudest possessions.

• CLOSING THOUGHTS

"I swept the universe with my telescope," an astronomer observed, "and I found no God."

A medical student added, "I have dissected a cadaver; I've opened every organ of the human body, but in no place did I find a soul."

Both assert that since it cannot be seen in a microscope or with a telescope, since it cannot be subjected to empirical testing, what is called the "spiritual" component of life cannot be authentic.

We sometimes tend to dismiss the spiritual side of life, and are often suspicious of—even uncomfortable with—the notion of personal religious experience. Concepts like "soul" and "spirituality" seem farfetched: too irrational, too unscientific, too fuzzy to be taken seriously.

Research for this book has led the authors to conclude that the spiritual side of life is absolutely real. Human beings are far more than electrical impulses, more than the sum of our chemical ingredients, and certainly more than thinking machines.

We asked Rabbi Abner Bergman of Temple Judea of Manhasset, New York, to respond to the naysayers.

To the astronomer, who by looking into his telescope concluded that there was no God in the universe, I would answer, "That makes as much sense as my saying that I took apart my violin, examined each piece, and could find no melody.'"

To the medical student, who said he couldn't find the human soul while dissecting the body, I'd respond, "When you opened the brain, did you find a thought? When you opened the heart, did you find a feeling of love? When you dissected the eye, did you discover a vision?" Yet we know very well that thoughts, feelings, and visions do indeed exist. We know that these things are real because we experience them to be real, though they may or may not be susceptible to scientific proof.

The rabbi offered another example.

When a musician looks at a piece of music, he analyzes the harmonic structure and the rhythm of the composition. When a scientist thinks of that same piece, she thinks of sound waves, frequencies, the minute structure of the inner ear, electrical impulses, and synapses. But when they are alone with one another, hear that same piece of music, and gaze romantically into the other's eyes, each says, "They're playing our song!"

When we speak of spiritual experience, we mean experience that deepens our feeling of connectedness to the world and to other people. What we call spiritual experience may or may not occur in a specific religious setting or context, but it is indeed religious experience.

chapter seven

"Is This What I Wanted to Be When I Grew Up?"

Coping with Work When Routine Replaces the Dream

"Nothing is really work unless you would rather be doing something else."
—Sir James Bame

how come i feel so disconnected
if this is such a user-friendly world?

144

F or many people, work offers the only place to experience a feeling of belonging to something outside the family. Because we spend more time there (2,000 hours a year!) than we do with our friends and neighbors, it's important for the workplace to supply us with more than "just a job." Our work determines our level of income and standard of living. It defines our identity and describes who we are (what do you do?). It is one of the principal means through which we can make a contribution and see life as worthwhile. Ninety percent of us are employees working for companies, government agencies, and nonprofit concerns. How we treat each other from 9 to 5, how purposefully we spend our energy, how clearly we understand the way what we do fits into the whole picture, will determine what kind of workplace we deserve.

We are moving away from working in arenas that support rigid pyramid-style hierarchies and moving toward working environments that regard us as valued, respected, integral parts of a team. It's becoming clearer that our life and our work are not mutually exclusive. Seventy percent of us earning over $30,000 a year would give up a day's pay for a day off.[1] Twenty percent of us who called in sick this year did so because we needed the time to relax.[2] Challenge and growth, fulfillment and leisure are giving salary raises and prestige a run for the money as the most coveted perks of the '90s.

Today more of us are looking for recognition, praise, transfer of skills, and an opportunity to learn from our work. Because so few can be promised rapid advancement and swift salary increases, we'll accept flexibility, more training, and some fun instead. We want to know what's going on in the firm and that what we think matters. Those who say they're most satisfied with their jobs are involved in decision making and encouraged to take calculated risks.

Another factor in job satisfaction is the bond created between coworkers. While it might not guarantee intimacy, daily contact certainly facilitates friendship. Studies show that individuals achieve more and stay longer in jobs where they enjoy relationships that share a basic understanding of their daily pressures and concerns.[4] When people work together, what they share in common—shop talk about job crises and successes, comforts, and hazards—gives them the opportunity to offer practical help and emotional support. When organizations foster this camaraderie through company policy and a physical environment that encourages frequent interaction, everyone benefits.

A century ago, most people viewed work not as an end in itself but as a means to an end, to provide for the family. What people did for a living was an instrument of purpose, not itself a provider of

Reality Check–On the Job, It's Praise, Not Raise

A 1994 survey by Robert Half International, a staffing services firm, suggests that companies are in danger of losing good workers if they do not learn to nourish egos with warm adjectives and admiring nouns. The poll of 150 executives from the nation's 1,000 largest companies found the single most common reason that employees left was lack of recognition and praise.[3]

how come i feel so disconnected
if this is such a user-friendly world?

146

purpose. Today more of us seek a sense of purpose in our work. We want to feel we are striving toward something important, that we are immersed in something bigger than ourselves. If we can find that purposefulness in our work—because our company is the best in its field, active in civic and humanitarian causes, or committed to producing a quality product—then we might be willing to barter this meaning for monetary compensations.

If we figure out what we want from work, it will be easier to find out how to get it. We might need to learn new skills to increase our marketability. Or it might be a matter of evaluating our priorities and refocusing energies in new ways. But if we can find a workplace in which we trust the people we work for, have pride in what we do, and enjoy the people we are working with, then we will not have to come up with the solution alone.

When what you do seems too far removed from your passions, values, and beliefs, change your expectations.

In a perfect world we'd be paid more than we knew how to spend. Our work would entail no drudgery and would provide loads of opportunities for self-fulfillment. What we did would make a worthwhile contribution to humanity. Unfortunately, if many of us had to rate the basics of work on a scale from 1 to 10, our satisfaction with the work itself, our salary, the people we work with, the workplace itself, the product or service we provide, the company, the hours and perks, and the outlook for the future might be less than we'd desire.

(text continues on page 151)

True or False in Today's Workplace?

Here's a quiz designed to rankle and file. See how well you figure out what's up and what's not, what's coming and what's gone forever in today's workplace.

1. A woman who makes it to the top of the company is likely to act more like the men who reach the same heights than like women further down the corporate food chain.

2. Over 60 percent of American workers have been with their current employer for less than five years.

3. A recent survey of retail shops across America revealed "good pay" as the number one reason employees chose to work there.

4. "Excessive work hours" is the most contentious work-family issue in most dual-career homes.

5. As a rule, CEOs are dissatisfied with their jobs.

6. Small businesses have been hit hard by the enforcement of the Family and Medical Leave Act that guarantees up to twelve weeks of unpaid leave a year for family medical emergencies.

7. In the past twenty years the proportion of retired men in the 56–64 age group has more than doubled.

8. Companies earning healthy profits are less likely to cut costs than those that are struggling.

9. Most CEOs get ready for the work day by reading the business news section of the newspaper first and listening to the nationally broadcast Bloomberg Business News on the radio on their way to the office.

10. The conflict between our jobs as employees and our roles as parents has been said to be the single largest source of stress in the United States today.

11. Americans have less time off from work each year than do workers in England, France, and Sweden.

how come i feel so disconnected
if this is such a user-friendly world?

148

12. Fewer than half of all employees say they have an "excellent" or "good" relationship with their boss.

13. Most high-achieving working women believe they are paid what they're worth.

14. Women are more successful at apple polishing, courting favors, exuding charm, using wiles, and flattering the boss than men are.

15. A recent study conducted by the Commonwealth Fund found that productivity and profits increased and turnover dropped when workers over 55 were hired.

16. Given the choice, most employees will trade wages and benefits for flexibility and autonomy.

17. Conflicts between work and family tend to be resolved in favor of the family.

18. Younger workers are more likely to be personally prepared to work in a racially and technically diverse environment than older workers.

ANSWERS

1. **False.** A *Harvard Business Review* study of 456 female executives revealed that men and women use very different leadership styles. Men prefer a "command-and-control" style in dealing with subordinates— relying on orders, appeals to self-interest, rational decision making, and rewards. Women prefer to work "interactively"— sharing power and information, motivating by appeals to organizational goals, and promoting empowerment.[5]

2. **True.** Sixty-two percent of American workers have been with their current employer for less than five years. In Japan, by contrast, only 37 percent of workers have been with their current employer for less than five years.[6]

3. **False.** When 13,000 employees in retail shops across America were asked to list in order the 18 reasons for working where they

did, they ranked "good pay" third. In first place was "appreciation of work done," with "respect for me as a person" second.[7]

4. **False.** Job-generated pressure, which spills over at home in the form of preoccupation, fatigue, and irritability, created more arguments than excessive work hours.[8]

5. **True.** Seventy-five percent are looking for a better job! The survey, conducted by the Cornell University Center for Advanced Human Resource Studies, showed that 75 percent of those surveyed had conducted some type of job inquiry or had begun to explore job opportunities in the previous twelve months and that 58 percent actually had initiated contacts with other employers about a job.[9]

6. **False.** There has been little impact on small business because so few employees have taken advantage of the new leave entitlement. Two thirds of employers covered by an earlier California leave law reported that less than one percent of their employees had taken a leave.[10]

7. **True.** This group has grown from 15 percent to 32 percent, mainly because large corporations have been shedding their older, more expensive middle managers.[11]

8. **False.** Hard times have always forced firms of every size to cut costs, but recent job cuts have been at companies earning healthy profits. Jobs are disappearing not just on the factory floor, as was so often the case in the past, but among the managers and professionals who have traditionally comprised the heart and soul of large firms. And big firms are shedding jobs not merely to cut costs, but also to change the very way they are managed.[12]

9. **False.** Only 2 percent of 3,100 presidents and vice presidents of Fortune 1000 companies read the business news first. A third head

how come i feel so disconnected
if this is such a user-friendly world?

150

straight to the sports section, a fifth to the lifestyle pages, and about a fifth to the front page. And 41 percent of them are listening to Howard Stern![13]

10. **True.** 'Nuff said![14]

11. **True.** The typical American gets two weeks less vacation time than the typical British, French, or German worker, three and a half weeks less than the average Swede.[15]

12. **False.** A remarkable 81 percent of employees say they have a good or excellent relationship with their boss.[16]

13. **True.** Fifty-one percent of high-achieving career women believe they are paid what they're worth—although 27 percent said they'd get paid more if they were men.[17]

14. **False.** Apple polishing seems to pay off better for men. Those men who use the very ploys that backfire for women take home heftier salaries than those who don't. The more straightforward women are on the job, the better.[18]

15. **True.** The most significant finding of this report is the eagerness of older people to work and their ability to contribute. Changing government and industry policies to make it easier for older people to work would increase our gross national product and eliminate some of the drain on Social Security and Medicare.[19]

16. **True.** Most workers want more time for themselves and their families and would like to spend less time working. They value benefits such as flexible time and dependent-care assistance, and, when they don't have them, they'd be willing to make tradeoffs for such programs.[20]

17. **False.** Unfortunately, conflicts tend to be resolved in favor of the job, usually to the detriment of the family and worker.[21]

18. **False.** Younger workers are no better prepared than older workers.[22]

The words we use to describe what we feel like when we're unhappy at work—burnout, hitting the wall, bottoming out, midlife crisis—are the same whether work is too boring or too demanding.

To avoid the frustration and stress that accompany an unsuccessful working day, we need to develop a new attitude. Here are some techniques to charge the enthusiasm that brings satisfaction to work:

• Stay absorbed in what you're doing. If you're there, be there—don't be a body on automatic pilot. Pay attention. If your mind wanders, note where it went and put those concerns on hold. If you stay focused in the present and intent on doing the best you can do, you won't be thinking about watching the minutes tick by.

• Believe in the importance of what you're doing. If your job seems insignificant, take the time to explore the operational dynamics of your company; find out just

> *"The only place where success comes before work is in the dictionary."*
> —*Vidal Sassoon*

where your part fits in. When you recognize that your contribution is a key piece in the puzzle, you'll see that your job matters. Then put your heart into doing your personal best.

• Establish rituals. Be aware of what's involved in how you start your day, tidy up, take breaks, and organize yourself. Take advantage of this knowledge to focus and center yourself.

• Maintain a balance between concern and the lack of it in situations that don't work out the way you intended. Ride the waves. Analyze your failures, and then go back to the beginning and start over. Remember: what's inherently satisfying in work are the challenges we master.

how come i feel so disconnected
if this is such a user-friendly world?

152

- De-emphasize the product and focus on the process. View your problems at work as an opportunity to learn more and to think creatively. What can you learn in the course of your everyday work about the equipment you use? About your fellow workers and clients? About the businesses you interact with? What can be done to humanize? Streamline? Unclog bottlenecks? What's the best time of day to talk to your boss? How should you prepare? Studying problems and keeping an open mind can lead directly to improving your circumstances at work.

- Find your natural rhythms at work. Anything that brings rhythm—tension and relaxation, effort and breakthrough—balances your workday and refreshes your attitude toward it. Take time out from any continuous task to vary it with another. Like the natural rhythms of breathing in and out, sleeping and waking, workplace rhythms defray the negative effects of routine.

- Help someone else on the job. Take the time to ask a coworker, "What can I do to help?" You might be needed to share information, resources, creative ideas, or expert skills; to fill in for an absentee; or just to listen. A grateful coworker could become a forever friend.

- Allow yourself to relax and unwind. There are several simple focusing techniques (a personal favorite of the authors is Dr. Herbert Benson's *The Relaxation Response*) that can release frustration and stress when the pressure mounts. Once learned, they can work their magic in just minutes, returning a more relaxed you back to concentration and activity.

- Keep a sense of humor. Learn to laugh at your own follies, foibles, and mistakes. Break the ice at an awkward moment with a joke or lighthearted personal anecdote. By taking yourself less seriously, you'll lighten up not only your workplace but also your own spirits.

- If these suggestions for helping out a boring or overwhelming situation don't help at all, consider other work options. If you feel stuck, what about a lateral move? Just because your job is not giving you adequate opportunities to learn and grow doesn't mean other situations don't exist. Explore alternatives.[23]

Are you feeling taken for granted at work? Here are a few suggestions to increase the appreciation shown to you:

- Discuss your feelings with your boss. Cite specific incidents in which you felt overlooked or unrecognized.

Reality Check—What Do Workers Want?

It's simple. We want more control over our destiny, and we're willing to sacrifice cash and benefits for it. Our attitudes and aspirations are redefining success in terms of personal satisfaction and respect, autonomy, and open communication with our employer. We all have to survive today's turbulence of layoffs, restructuring, and an increasingly diverse workforce to get there, but get there we will.

Reasons people considered to be "very important" in deciding to take a job with their current employer:

Open communications, 65%

Effect on personal/family life, 60%

Nature of work, 59%

Management quality, 59%

Supervisor, 58%

Gain new skills, 55%

Control over work content, 55%

Job security, 54%

Co-worker quality, 53%

Stimulating work, 50%

Job location, 50%

Family-supportive policies, 46%

Fringe benefits, 43%

Control over work schedule, 38%

Advancement opportunity, 37%

Salary/wage, 35%

Access to decision makers, 33%

No other offers, 32%

Management opportunity, 26%

Size of employer, 18%

From *The National Study of the Changing Workforce.* Source: Families and Work Institute. Reprinted with permission.[24]

how come i feel so disconnected
if this is such a user-friendly world?

154

- Rely on coworkers as a support group. The boss is not the only one who can validate your importance; recognition from peers can be a great boost to your morale. Be willing to take the first step: compliment and congratulate your coworkers on jobs well done. By being supportive, you'll encourage them to reciprocate.

- Look for recognition outside the workplace. If you can't get what you need on the job, find sources of fulfillment in your personal life that will give you the applause you need.

- Look within. Review your own projects and achievements. Recognize your merits and accomplishments, and praise yourself for jobs well done. Remember: your ultimate source of appreciation is you.[25]

> "One of the saddest things is, the only thing a man can do for eight hours a day, day after day, is work. You can't eat eight hours a day, nor drink for eight hours a day, nor make love for eight hours."
> —William Faulkner

- AT A DEAD END? AFTER HOURS, THERE'S STILL HOPE Sad but true: sometimes you're stuck in a dead-end job that's a no-win, just plain rotten situation. And there's not much you can do in the workplace to make it more personally satisfying.

This is not a time to give up. Instead, you have to rebalance, refocus, and compensate after hours for what's missing.

- If your brain is undernourished and you're not intellectually stimulated by your job, charge your mental batteries in the evenings and on weekends by taking a course, attending a seminar, or joining a discussion group—on astrology or great classics, holistic health care or fine wine—any subject you've always wanted to learn more about.

- If you spend too many hours alone, behind a cubicle, in front of a computer, or inside a private office, get social after hours. Seek group activities that encourage conversation and interaction. How about an exercise class? Dinner out with some friends? Maybe a bowling league or card game?

- If creativity is in short supply, find creative outlets outside work. Take piano or painting lessons; sink your fingers into clay; sign up for a poetry class; buy a sketch pad and recreate scenes from your own backyard . . .

- If you're low man on the totem pole and feel like all you do every day is take orders, get involved in an activity that allows you to be the boss. Coach your daughter's soccer team; chair a committee at your local church or civic group; take charge and organize a ski trip or potluck dinner.

- If your muscles ache from sitting in the same chair for hours every day, get physical. Join a gym; sign up for a weekend softball or basketball league; call a friend and go out for a power walk. Or try a brand new activity—how about karate? Fencing? Rollerblading?

- If you face the boring "blahs" during working hours and feel more like a robot than a human, reward yourself for getting through a day. After hours, play hard. Challenge yourself with activities that allow some risk taking and let the steam out of the pressure cooker. What excites you—bungee jumping? Hang gliding? Scuba diving? Choose one play activity and do it!

- If you've lost your sense of purpose and can't find any meaning in your work, pick a cause and volunteer. Opportunities for feeling more worthwhile surround you: working with frail senior citizens or

how come i feel so disconnected
if this is such a user-friendly world?

156

developmentally disabled toddlers; becoming involved with environmental issues or the fight against AIDS; volunteering your time at a local soup kitchen or climbing on board to raise money for Cancer Care. Invest as little or as much time as you choose—and watch how quickly that aimlessness dissolves.

While after-hours options don't promise to improve the quality of your job, they will make you feel better inside and allow you to explore an alternate route around that dead end.

Don't work behind a closed door-keep in touch with the people you work with.

Just how important is congeniality in the workplace? Very, say corporate experts. Job satisfaction hinges on camaraderie, enjoyment, and even fun. If job satisfaction vanishes, hard work will soon disappear as well. When *Industry Week* surveyed its readers several years ago asking for "cures for what ails our organizations," the most frequently cited remedies were teamwork, recognition, and a boss who cares—all of which are readily available and would cost companies absolutely nothing. It's the human dimension that makes the difference between going to work and looking forward to going to work.[26]

You don't have to be a manager to emerge from your office or cubbyhole and show that you care. When was the last time you:

• Sent someone you work with a birthday, anniversary, or congratulations card?

- Called a coworker who was home sick, just to see how he or she was feeling?
- Brought someone in your workplace a cup of coffee—just because?
- Asked a coworker to see a photo of a new grandchild, pictures from his or her daughter's graduation, a wedding, or any recent special occasion?
- Said something nice and unsolicited to a coworker—anything from "What a great tan" to "I really like working with you"?
- Asked someone at work to have a drink or dinner after hours, meet for golf or tennis, go to the beach or a museum, take in a movie?

If your answer is "further back in time than I'd like to admit," it's time to make changes. The workplace walls are weak and just waiting to be crumbled.

Hungry for job satisfaction? Take a lunch break.

If taking a lunch break has become an exception rather than routine, it's time to stop cheating yourself of the midday "time out" that you deserve—and need.

Looking For The Boss . . . Is He Ever in His Office?

"That's the biggest complaint I get these days," admits George, a high school principal. *"But I take it as a compliment—that the teachers, parents, and kids realize I'm not locked behind closed doors but out there where things are happening, where my presence really counts. The administrating part of my job would be easier if I stayed in my office. But that's not where I belong; I belong in the classrooms, the cafeteria, the hallways, the gym—observing and listening and coming up with ways to make things run better.*

"In the cafeteria sometimes I grab an apron and help serve the lunches, taking advantage of those opportunities to talk to both the staff and students. In an advanced math class I sit and try to tackle problems—getting stumped with the best of the kids. My most productive times are wandering through the halls—talking to whoever's hanging around. The more visible I am, the more I hear and the more I learn. The more connected I become to the people who count, the better principal I can be."

how come i feel so disconnected
if this is such a user-friendly world?

158

For some of us who are busier than ever at work, time out for lunch has become an expendable luxury. But while we might be tempted to work straight through lunch hour and rationalize that we'll make it up with a big dinner, these decisions do us a disservice.

Because 1) physiologically we are ill equipped to work for eight hours without a break; 2) we are a reflection not only of what we eat but of how we eat it; and 3) the best gossip, advice, and secrets are shared during lunchtime, it is imperative that we make taking a lunch break a priority. Lunch may be the least important part of lunch time. While the burgers provide the protein, it's the conversation that stimulates the mind and the companionship that nurtures the soul.

When times get tough, keep the lines of communication open. Use the right words to get what you want.

When Mr. Spock of "Star Trek" wanted a perfect transfer of information between himself and a fellow Vulcan, he did a "mind meld." By touching skulls, he enabled the information to flow from his mind to another's—in a faultless process. If only Mr. Spock's skill was transferable to Planet Earth. . . .

Unfortunately, we've got to rely on our own flawed techniques to communicate—techniques that, when they break down, can result in serious misunderstandings. When the sailing's smooth, it's easy to say "thank you" or "job well done." But when what we say is more negative—when we are angry or confronting or critical—the challenge to express ourselves honestly, clearly, and kindly can be most daunting.

As angry as we may sometimes get, it's vital to accept and confront our feelings—and lethal not to, warns Gilda Carle, Ph.D., a corporate communications specialist based in Yonkers, New York. When people feel a loss of control, *anger* is just a *d* away from *danger*. Workers under stress have higher cholesterol levels than their colleagues who are less pressured.

A 1992 study of 700 men and women at the University of Michigan found that people who suppressed their anger were three times more likely to die prematurely than those who vented their frustration.[27]

Manage your anger. Were you passed over for a promotion by someone you personally trained? Did you take the rap for something a coworker botched? Were you not applauded for a project you poured your heart and soul into? To manage your anger, Dr. Carle offers these first three steps:

1. Frame it. Get up, get a grip, get moving. Run around the office building if necessary. Try writing a hateful letter to the person who wronged you—but don't send it!

Here's My Business Card; Pass the Sweet 'n Low

"When we first formed WIB (Women in Business) as a means to network with other women in neighboring towns, our most difficult task was deciding when to meet," says Shirley, the group's president and owner of an office supply business. *"We were twenty women with different schedules. Some wanted evenings; others said they had commitments or were too tired after work. A few suggested Saturday, but the moms in the group vetoed that. Finally we agreed to meet at lunchtime—12 noon, the first Wednesday of the month.*

"Each of us comes prepared with specific services to offer or request. When I'm looking for a new computer system and someone across the table in the computer business needs new file cabinets and office supplies—it's a collaboration made in heaven! We use our meetings to trade, barter, share information, and build relationships."

how come i feel so disconnected
if this is such a user-friendly world?

160

Mammograms and Manicures: TGIF for the "Lunch Team"

Betty, Pat, and Stacy have worked in the same office for three years—and have spent their lunch hour together every day for the last two. Known by the rest of the office as the "lunch team," they can be found in the company cafeteria Mondays and Wednesdays, at the health club a half mile away taking step classes on Tuesdays and Thursdays, and somewhere more fun on Fridays. Whether it's trying a new cuisine (Portuguese food was the latest), getting a manicure, or checking out the latest sales at Macy's—the weekend spirit begins to soar on Friday at noon.

The newest addition to their lunch schedule: yearly mammograms on the first Friday in June. "When I turned 40, my doctor told me it was time," explains Pat. "But I kept postponing that first visit. When I realized that neither Betty or Stacy had ever had one, that clinched it; we decided to go together. Now it's on the calendar—one less Friday of the year to plan."

2. Claim it. So you're angry—fine. Now take responsibility for doing something about it.

3. Tame it. Close your eyes and imagine the person who's the source of your anger standing behind thick Plexiglas. Put a picture frame around the person, and then distance yourself from that picture.

Once you've regained control, it's time for the fourth step—confrontation of the offender. Dr. Carle suggests:

• Give the person specific factual information about his/her behavior—without judging it. ("You yelled at me in the meeting in front of the entire department staff.")

• Explain the effect of this behavior on you. ("It makes me feel tense . . . frustrated . . . inadequate . . . embarrassed.") When you express your feelings in words, they are validated—feelings can't be wrong.

- Share your thoughts. Instead of pinning the blame ("You never listen to my ideas"), use a statement that begins with "I." ("I wish you would be more responsive," or "patient," "encouraging," or whatever.)
  - Explain what you need in the future—how can you work on this together?
  - End the confrontation—and don't bring it up again. Let go of the anger and open the door for healing.

Take the pain out of criticism. Put the word "constructive" before the process and redefine it as a positive experience.

The key to constructive criticism lies in choosing the right words—and in conveying them with respect.

Test yourself. If an employee continued to leave work earlier every day without letting you know, would you say:

A. "You always leave early without telling me; I resent your inconsiderate behavior," or

B. "I get upset when you don't tell me that you're planning to leave early because I depend on you to get specific tasks done."

How about a self-centered coworker who monopolizes planning meetings with irrelevant personal monologues—would you tell him:

A. "You irritate me when you talk about personal matters, waste everybody's time, and foul up our schedule," or

B. "When you spend undue time on nonbusiness conversations, I'm concerned because we don't meet our schedules."

how come i feel so disconnected
if this is such a user-friendly world?

162

When options are given, the choice is easy. But for situations where there are no A and B from which to pick, here are some guidelines:

1. Choose the right time. While the incident is fresh in your mind but when you feel the person is ready to hear what you have to say, provide feedback face to face and in private.

2. Be positive. Couch the criticism with a compliment. "You know how much I value your work here but . . ." "I know how hard you worked on that report but . . ."

3. Be specific. Address the behavior, not the person. Not "You're inconsiderate, lazy, etc. . . ." but "You left early three days without telling anyone" or "You missed two deadlines when you took the afternoon off." Don't bring up past problems regarding other issues, but stick to the immediate problem.

4. Be objective. Report the facts. Instead of "You were pouting during the meeting," try "You didn't respond to any of my questions during the meeting."

5. Be a witness, not a judge. Focus not on blaming, but on what would be useful to do in the future. Try to agree to constructive changes. Then quit while you're both ahead![28]

Open up on the receiving end. Learn to accept criticism, not as an attack on your ego, but as an opportunity to learn.

It's never easy to hear that we've goofed, disappointed, or fallen short. Even a well-intended, perfectly executed confrontation can leave us feeling attacked.

How to soften the blow? Start by repeating these "Mantras for Accepting Criticism":

1. I am not my mistake.

2. It's OK to dislike my behavior and still like myself. I am not a bad person because I goofed.

3. I am responsible for my actions. I can modify, improve, correct, or defend them.

Calmer and collected, we are better armed to respond appropriately. Start by asking yourself: Was the criticism unjustified? Were you told that you're always late, when in fact you've been late twice in the past three years? If you think so, you might say:

- "I don't agree with you, but I'd like to work this out."

- "I understand how you might see it that way, but I don't share your perception."

- "It seems you're displeased with my behavior. Could you give me more specific examples?"

Was the criticism valid? If so, the best response is to admit your mistake or shortcoming:

- "You're right; I did do that incorrectly. Now that I understand how, I'll complete it correctly."

- "I understand what you're saying. Do you have any suggestions as to how I could improve?"

- "I'm sorry you're disappointed in me; I'd like to work this out with you."

Naturally, each confrontation is unique, and responses will vary based on the nature of the situation. The bottom line in breaking the

how come i feel so disconnected
if this is such a user-friendly world?

164

tension is to keep the lines of communication open and work continuously to stay connected.[29]

Take your turn; be a mentor. Adopt a protege and show him or her the ropes.

Who first taught you how to throw a ball? Drive a car? Who helped prepare you for your first job interview? With your first job assignment?

Over the years, it's been the mentors in our lives who have showed us how to make it, taken us under their wings, and guided us with the benefit of their experience. Their rewards—feelings of being needed, of being respected, admired, and followed, of making a difference—make the relationship between mentor and "mentoree" one of life's mutually beneficial partnerships.

> "By working faithfully eight hours a day you may eventually get to be a boss and work 12 hours a day."
> —Robert Frost

Mentoring has caught on as an important business management tool. As companies recognize its value, CEOs are encouraging mentoring relationships. Only a small number of companies have formal mentoring programs. Many more have informal arrangements between fledglings and more experienced advisers who volunteer to share their knowledge and experience.

Why mentor? For both new recruits and their mentors, the alliance brings about a unity of purpose and a team spirit that no formal training can provide. It's an opportunity for mentors to share in-house experience and information that's not available in any classroom. Perhaps most important, it's a feeling of security for a novice who never has to feel alone or abandoned. If he fails or stumbles, he's got someone to lean on.

Ask yourself—to whom have I offered a helping hand lately? If the answer is "no one":

1. Adopt a novice in your workplace. Choose someone you believe has talent, who needs guidance and can benefit from your knowledge and experience—and who wants a mentor!

2. Don't worry about formalities. There's no written contract here—it's an intangible arrangement that grows with time, based on how the day-to-day bond develops.

3. Share your experiences. Personal anecdotes are always welcome—both success stories and, more importantly, your mistakes.

4. Be a cheerleader. Your encouragement and reassurance will instill confidence in your protege, while your high standards will bring out her best. We can accept criticism when we know there's a helping hand or a gentle hug behind it.

5. Ask questions. "Why do you think you should . . . ?" "Who would be the best to . . . ?" "Where could you find information on . . . ?" "How can you do it better than . . . ?" The better you do your job as mentor, the faster your protege will become less needy of your guidance. Unlike a love affair, the best mentor relationship ends not in marriage but in separation.[30]

By generously sharing your expertise, you become the recipient of the soul-satisfying knowledge that you are making a difference by reaching out to help.

how come i feel so disconnected
if this is such a user-friendly world?

166

For those who work from home: fight the isolation. Keep in contact with the outside world.

Isn't it great working from home, not having to put on a tie or stockings every morning? Isn't it terrific not having to sit in a car for two hours during a torturous daily commute? Not having anyone standing over you while you work? No memos to assail you, meetings to interrupt you . . . ?

So what if you miss the office gossip, the latest jokes? So what if no one notices your new haircut, your ten-pound-thinner physique, or your new outfit? And what's the big deal if you start talking to your fax machine—and waiting for it to answer?

OK, so maybe working from home is not the perfect alternative. For the 32 million (up from 25 million in 1990!) who have chosen to telecommute or run a home-based business, isolation and loneliness can be serious hurdles to overcome.[31] All the little things that come naturally in the workplace—conversation, companionship, camaraderie—don't just happen by themselves when you work alone; you have to make them happen. Keeping in contact with the outside world is easier if you:

• Get out of the house. Make at least two appointments a week a mandatory part of your schedule.

• Join a business organization, professional guild, or networking or support group—and attend regular meetings.

• Reward yourself for a job completed with some form of personal contact. A project completed or report submitted? How about a well-deserved 15-minute chat on the phone with a friend or a half-hour walk with an exercise buddy?

• Enjoy the freedom. Take advantage of the flexibility and build pleasing activities into the day. An hour at the gym, a haircut, a karate lesson, even a midday movie can maximize your schedule and make it work effectively for you.

• DO UNTO OTHERS AS THEY WOULD HAVE YOU DO UNTO THEM

To change our answer to the question "What do you do?" from "I am an editor who happens to work for ABC Corporation right now," to "I work for ABC Corporation as an editor," business is going to have to keep us informed and involved.

Nineties buzzwords—interdependent networks, open communication, commonly created vision statements, respect for individual differences—will all help, and so will the acknowledgment that work and life are not separate concepts. When we asked the participants in our survey for an experience they'd consider a successful attempt by their workplace to instill a feeling of community, this is what we heard:

Employee stock ownership. "Hands down, the day my company instituted a program giving us all a share in the business. Now I feel we really are on the same team. Today if I'm asked to work harder for the sake of productivity and profitability, it's no longer a one-sided deal."

how come i feel so disconnected
if this is such a user-friendly world?

168

Health maintenance. "My company administers monthly pulmo-nary tests in behalf of a zero tolerance smoking policy. They installed automated health monitors, used in private stalls and activated by our thumbprint, that permit a variety of tests without going to a health facility. My good health is in their best interests, I realize, but I can't help feeling more valued for my own sake now."

Brainstorming meetings. "I just participated in my first one. Not only does the boss want to find out what I believe our problems are, but he's encouraging us to design solutions. When management gets out of the way and lets us put our suggestions into practice—that's a real community."

Moving up together. "My company fosters a network of personal ties. They subscribe to the theory that when people are part of a group, they achieve more and stay longer in businesses. So they like to hire more than one person at a time and let them move up through the ranks together. I was hired with three guys and we've all stayed close—never feeling like we're competing against one another but rooting each other on."

Fun at work. "Nothing engenders allegiance more than knowing you're going to have a good time at work. Bosses know that people who don't enjoy their jobs demand more money. My textile company gets us out of the office at least once a month. We've had meetings in art galleries, parks, and museums. We once went to a movie matinee. We all pitch in and decorate the office Christmas tree and celebrate birthdays, milestones, and accomplishments quarterly. Sometimes the ideas are a bit off the wall, but laughter spurs creativity and enthusiasm—as well as loyalty."

● CLOSING THOUGHTS

Some years ago, there was a group of brilliant young men at the University of Wisconsin. They were writers—all would-be poets, novelists, and essayists—extraordinary in their literary talents. These promising young men met regularly to read and critique each other's work. They were merciless with one another—demanding, rigid, and extremely tough in their criticism. The sessions became such arenas of literary judgment that the members of this exclusive club called themselves the "Stranglers."

Not to be outdone, the women of literary talent at the university started their own group. They called themselves the "Wranglers." They too read their works to each other. But there was one big difference: the criticism was softer, more positive, more encouraging and supportive. Every effort, even the most feeble, was encouraged.

The Little Things Show a Boss Cares

"My very first boss was my role model," says Sandra, now a boss herself. *"We were an office of twenty employees, and every morning our boss greeted each of us by name. He always remembered the details of our personal lives. If someone's husband had surgery, he knew. If someone's daughter just left for college, he asked how she was doing. He knew when we took our vacations, when it was our birthdays, when one of our kids was sick. The powerful memory of how that made us feel has stayed with me always.*

"Now that I own my own business I've made it a top priority to have that personal contact with my staff. I make sure to speak to each employee every day—not only to say good morning and good night, but to remember special occasions and ask about their personal lives. I want them to see me not only as their boss, but also as someone who cares."

how come i feel so disconnected
if this is such a user-friendly world?

170

Twenty years later, an alumnus of the University of Wisconsin was doing a study of his former classmates' careers, when he noticed a vast difference in the professional accomplishments of the Stranglers as compared to the Wranglers. Of all the bright young men, not one had made a significant literary contribution. From the Wranglers, however, had come six published authors—some nationally renowned!

So it is with us in our workplaces. As we soften our judgments and instead empower, support, encourage, and accept, we grow and enable those around us to grow. And as we show our appreciation to our coworkers, as we share and mentor and reward, we polish whatever goods we're producing with meaning and pride.

chapter eight

"I Need Some Quiet So I Can Remember What My Different Drummer Sounds Like"

Nourishing Your Soul– The Ultimate Connection

"What lies behind us and what lies before us are tiny matters when compared to what lies within us."
—William Morrow

how come i feel so disconnected
if this is such a user-friendly world?

172

Today we have more free time and more choice of how to fill that time than any civilization in history. Yet many of us are uncomfortable with being alone with our thoughts. It's as if we need permission to withdraw, as if nourishing our souls is not a good enough reason to find the time to look inward. Although millions of people travel and exercise, have hobbies and compete in sports, these activities are less playful and restorative than structured and goal directed. We take a bath, then earn that bath break by listening to an instructional book on tape. We play golf, and watch increasing numbers of players bring along their cellular phones to return a few calls between holes.

Even the custom of observing a day of recuperation once a week is dead. Sunday, until recently enforced through blue laws as a common day of rest, is now a frenzy of consumer activity. Nobody seems to mind. If it's good for the economy and convenient for those who work during the week, so what if the quiet time we're losing has helped preserve our health and sanity for centuries?

More than we're aware of, our minds and bodies need a break from the pressure and pace of daily life. All week long we spend and expend.

What we need to do is to install an errand-free, mall-free, task-free zone in our lives. For a few hours a week we can try to balance out the basic rhythm of life . . . supply some rest to our constant movement, add some *not* doing to our doing. We cheat ourselves if we never give a moment to contemplating our origin, our destiny, and our aspirations—if we never silently look inward.

This is true no matter how old we are or how much money we make. We have a tendency to focus on attaining our goals and then to lose our concentration when it comes to enjoying the accomplishment. Ask anyone going through a crisis, and they'll recall the moment before the crisis: the sweetness of everyday life, the sanctity of the ordinary, the preciousness of the mundane.

The aim here is to impress on you the importance of incorporating time to mull and to wonder. Then maybe you'll agree with artist Grant Wood, who said, "All the really good ideas I ever had came to me while I was milking a cow."

Discover your passion. What excites and energizes you? Dig deep to find your sources of pleasure.

There are 86,400 seconds in every day, and it's up to each of us to use them in the best way possible. If you don't wake up every morning with excitement to face the day, something is wrong. Too often we get so caught up in seeking balance in our lives that our passions are sacrificed for the sake of the larger picture. It's our responsibility to find what things in life will quicken our heartbeat—and make life happen.

What turns you on? Bird watching? Parasailing? Collecting stamps? Writing poetry? Listening to Mozart? If you've discovered your passion—or passions—bravo! You are envied by many. If you

how come i feel so disconnected
if this is such a user-friendly world?

174

Who Would Ever Think . . .

"What's your passion?" Predictably, among those we surveyed with this question, the health-conscious, physically fit men and women talked about golf and tennis; artists spoke of painting retreats; musicians were energized while composing or performing. But every now and then, just like passion itself, the answers surprised us.

- *"Rollerblading," says Katy, a 43-year-old stockbroker whose three-piece suit doesn't match the blades under her desk. "My 15-year-old son taught me how to rollerblade last year, and I can't stop. Not only is it great exercise, but it's the best way that I've ever found to release stress for a half hour during lunch time."*

- *"Working with the kids at the school for Down's syndrome," says Roger, a 22-year-old graduate student. "I started working there for course credit, one day a week. But the kids got under my skin. When the course was over, I kept going—now twice a week. There's no place I feel more special than when I'm with those kids."*

- *"Drag car racing," says Phil, a 50-year-old Monday-to-Friday accountant and weekend racer. "My life most of the time is as straight as an arrow, and pretty boring. Drag racing is my high. It's an instant rush—a way to get away from everything. When I race my 1969 red Camaro that I've had since college, I'm a different person."*

take time regularly to indulge those passions—even better. But if you're feeling passion-less or out of touch with what makes you sing . . .

Take a peek into your heart. Think about the times you've felt most energized. Where were you? What were you doing? Are you turned on by physical activity or tranquility? Would you get more excited by rock climbing or by meditating on top of one of the rocks? Is there something you've always wanted to try but never have? If you could be doing anything at this very moment, what would it be?

Don't be afraid to experiment. While some people discover their passions naturally, others may have to dabble before finding the source of their fervor. Let us not forget the truism: you never know until you try.

Give yourself permission to indulge your passions. Remember: those precious 86,400 seconds are ticking away too quickly. If we don't make the deep-down important things in life happen, we have only ourselves to blame.

Be realistic. Don't overdo. If you threw yourself into everything you did, life would just be too exhausting.

Try the do-it-yourself therapy of journal writing. It's a good way to get in touch with inner feelings.

Keeping a journal is an effective way of tuning into that "inner voice" of intuition. At its most basic level the act of writing in a journal gives you a chance to discover what you believe. This therapeutic ally can be a place to store feelings that might be too intense, puzzling, or private to be shared with another person. Journal writing can help you see various sides of a situation—and alternatives to consider.

After a few moments of writing in a journal, politeness and censors no longer cover up what you're actually feeling. You begin to penetrate what your mind is seeing—not what it's thinking it should be seeing. Sometimes what it sees is a glimpse of the hundred

how come i feel so disconnected
if this is such a user-friendly world?

176

Getting to Know Myself Better

"When I'm bored or unclear as to why I'm feeling isolated, writing helps put a label on what's bothering me," says Susan, a 44-year-old who has been keeping a journal for the last twelve years. *"How can I know what I think until I look at what I've said? When I read what I've written in the past, I can see patterns of other times when I've felt the same way. It's comforting to see that I've handled these down times before and that they always eventually pass.*

"I write every day for ten minutes, at the same time, in the same place, on my bed. Sometimes what comes out is last night's most vivid dream or an idea for my next project at work. Sometimes it's an old memory that's resurfaced or what I'm most afraid will happen tomorrow. I never edit, censor, or correct a thing. What a pleasure to be able to spend time undirected, uncontrolled, without the possibility of doing anything wrong—and at the same time, getting to know myself better."

separate people living under your skin. This chance to witness the inner workings of your mind is available when you give yourself the opportunity to listen to the space around you. Just acknowledging all your alter egos can be enough to renew your perception of who you are.

Rarely does writing down your thoughts lead directly to enlightenment. Rather, it's the accumulation of random ideas—as individual in length and content as a fingerprint—that often reveals solutions. A memory. A wish list. A nightmare. Jot them down and watch where they might lead you. All can facilitate an unexpected insight that gives you the momentum to move forward and take the next step in your life.

Here are some suggestions to jump-start your writing and help make the blank page less intimidating. Have patience. The fruits of these honest labors might take a while to ripen. But the reward will be fresh, healthy, and worthwhile.

Make a list of:
- the foods you hated most as a kid
- the best things a person could say about you
- your obsessions
- the things that come to mind to finish the sentence, "I remember . . ."
- activities you used to love but haven't done in a long time
- movies and books that have changed your life
- places you will never, ever go
- the secrets you keep from those you love
- the skills you've never tried but would love to master
- the reasons you want to keep a journal

Describe:
- your grandfather
- your day, in detail, before lunch today
- the most beautiful place you've ever visited
- an article of clothing you once loved
- a time you were caught lying
- your earliest memory
- when you've felt closest to nature
- the animal you most resemble
- what you do when you feel lonely
- a meal you love

Don't:
- be logical
- worry about spelling, punctuation, grammar, margins
- buy an expensive notebook or pen

how come i feel so disconnected
if this is such a user-friendly world?

178

- write too much initially
- be afraid to take a class in journal writing
- stop thinking of yourself as interesting
- give up on the opportunity to spend time learning more about yourself[1]

Redefine your idea of fitness. It's not only about sweating; it's also about enhancing your internal connections.

Admittedly, sweating is still in and exercise is definitely not on the way out. But the newest fitness programs are adding a new dimension of serenity to their sweat workouts. Last decade's slogans of "feel the burn" and "no pain, no gain," are being replaced by the terms "centering" and "balance." The '80s attitude of "just do it" has yielded to the '90s mantra of "It's how you do it." For fitness workouts, that translates into less strenuous, less competitive sessions, with the added discipline of mind expansion.

Relax . . . and welcome to New Age Fitness—a holistic approach that draws on philosophies and practices from both the west and the east to view the concept of health as wholeness, perfection, and balance of body and mind.[2]

Holistic healers, in their practices, draw from a range of natural therapies to achieve physical, emotional, intellectual, and spiritual well-being. But you don't have to be hurting to benefit from many of these techniques. For a continued healthy and fit body and mind, prevention is the best medicine. Maybe that's why in ancient China many doctors were paid only as long as they kept their patients healthy. When a patient became sick, payment stopped—for as long as it took until the patient recovered. The motivation for a speedy recovery was a salary resumed—a system nothing like we in America know today, but surely a logical plan to encourage good health.

Staying holistically fit is an ongoing process, says Steven Schenkman, President of The New Center for Wholistic Health, Education and Research in Syosset, New York. Here are some of his suggestions for staying in balance.

Eat your way to better health. Making the transition from a diet of fast food and junk food to one that's low in fat and high in fiber is an important first step in promoting health, minimizing disease, and staying fit.

Stay in touch. There are a number of different techniques to manipulate muscles and soft tissue that not only help to relax you but also redirect the flow of energy to improve your well-being. You may feel like you're pampering yourself with a therapeutic massage or an AMMA therapy session (a complex system of hands-on treatment; in Chinese, *AMMA* means push-pull), but you're also helping yourself to stay fit.

Get a periodic spinal tune-up. The chiropractic system is based on the premise that the spine is literally the backbone of human health—and misalignments of the vertebrae can result in pressure on the spinal cord, leading to diminished function or illness. A monthly adjustment (with any necessary manipulation) by a licensed chiropractor can correct most misalignments and promote fitness.

how come i feel so disconnected
if this is such a user-friendly world?

180

Self Revelations: Nurturing Our Closest Relationship

When we asked those we surveyed who scheduled time for solitude into their lives to describe the benefits of this "zoning out" time, here is what they said:

- *"It gives me a chance to develop a sense of perspective—to recognize my imperfections and learn to better accept criticism."*
- *"After a personal disappointment or failure, some time alone with myself reminds me that success in life doesn't depend on just one event."*
- *"It gives me a chance to judge whether the way I behaved in a given situation was really to help myself or to hurt someone else . . . and it forces me to face the truth."*
- *"It forces me to concentrate on the gaps in my life . . . the things I'd like to understand better or have more control over."*
- *"It's my chance to think seriously about the hard questions, like what contribution I'd like to make in this lifetime."*
- *"It allows me the chance to review and better understand a recent experience."*

Go with the flow. Stimulate your body's healing energy with an exercise that balances the flow of vital life energy. Highly disciplined movements and forms are thought to unite body and mind and bring balance to your life. "External" methods like karate and judo stress endurance and muscular strength, while "internal" methods such as tai chi and aikido stress relaxation and control. Explore these disciplines and stick with the one that makes you feel best.

Take control to reduce your stress. There's more than one way to do it; techniques vary widely in style, but the goal is the same: stress reduction. You may want to try some of the following techniques.

- Biofeedback: Consciously visualizing yourself relaxing, while observing light, sound, or metered feedback, helps you adjust toward a more balanced internal state.
- Aromatherapy: Essential oils are massaged into the skin, inhaled, or placed in a bath to reduce stress and anxiety.
- Zero balancing: A method of touch akin to acupressure overcomes imbalances beneath the level of conscious awareness to realign body structure and body energy.
- Yoga: These exercises often concentrate on achieving perfection in posture and body alignment to gain mental control and access to higher consciousness.
- Relaxation response: By practicing two basic steps—the repetition of a word or short phrase, and a gentle return to the repetition whenever distracting thoughts occur—you can trigger a series of physiological changes (lower heart rate, lower breathing rate) that offer protection against stress.

This is just a beginning. The bottom line to staying holistically fit is to become—and remain—a full participant in your own health care.[3]

Unstructure some time to take a walk, gaze out a window, or sit on a park bench.

Writer May Sarton called solitude "the salt of personhood . . . that brings out the authentic flavor of every experience." In theory we might respect the notion that alone time is important, but too many of us really don't believe it. For some reason we find people who

how come i feel so disconnected
if this is such a user-friendly world?

182

enjoy keeping to themselves—who actually like their own company—suspicious. There seems to be an anxiety about becoming more conscious, going off automatic pilot, and thinking without distraction. Instead of viewing solitude as an opportunity to be wholly what we are, to feel whatever we feel absolutely, the world tries to convince us we have better things to do with our time.

Those who have grown comfortable with a life crammed full of "stuff" to do view solitude as they do daydreaming, procrastinating, lollygagging, or goofing off. If too many of us agree, time to just "be" will become an endangered pastime.

Psychologists and sociologists find this time to savor the silence to be emotionally vital. It helps us sort out life's complications and generates creative ideas. It's not idleness; it's an opportunity to let the world fall away so your true self can emerge.

In solitude we can explore what's most meaningful to us, free from other people's expectations. If we compulsively busy ourselves—viewing time alone as an expendable luxury—we run the risk of defining ourselves through others.

Let your "natural parent" be your guide to a closer connection with your soul. Get back to basics with Mother Nature.

Nature-oriented travel has become the fastest-growing segment of the tourism industry.[4] Thoreau had the right idea: communion with the earth is therapy for the psyche. Nothing can compare to experiencing firsthand the natural wonders of the earth. The total sensory experience promises to illuminate your spirit.

Opportunities for "earth adventures" are vast—from a simple hour of snorkeling among coral reefs to a challenging one-month Himalayan trek to Mount Everest; from an adventurous river-rafting expedition to a serene walk on cross-country skis through a snowy countryside; from a research expedition assisting an archaeologist to a moment of meditation on top of a mountain.

Before you embrace Mother Nature, however, consider:

• What are your time constraints?

• How much money do you have to spend?

Outward Bound . . . And Better Than Ever

"I don't know what possessed me to venture into the wilderness," says Emily, who prefers hotels to camping, hates bugs, and is terrified of bears. "A friend got me at a weak moment, and off we went to Outward Bound, a wilderness program that promised to make a difference in our lives.

"There we were—me and nature—rappelling down cliffs, paddling down rapids, using muscles I never knew I had. I was a wreck before each activity, intimidated by every new challenge. Luckily, we were kept so busy, I had no time to think about my dirty apartment, the problems I was having with my boyfriend, or the project due at work two days after I returned home.

"As the days passed, I became more comfortable and confident. I found myself leading the way to the top of the hill and helping others in the group climb over the rocks and paddle to lunch. For the first time in my life I felt like a leader. Never before was I so energized. By the end of the week my friend was calling me Rocky.

"Even though I lost the high the minute I got back to work, the knowledge of what I had physically accomplished and the awareness of how much stronger I am than I ever imagined will stay with me always. The program kept its promise . . . it made a lasting difference in my life."

how come i feel so disconnected
if this is such a user-friendly world?

184

- What level of participation do you want to undertake—physically and mentally?
- Do you want to travel alone or with a group?
- Do you want to travel by cruise ship, plane, jeep, canoe, camel, bus, bike, raft, or foot?
- What do you want to see? Plants? Animals? Cultures?
- What do you want to learn?[5]

Then cast aside all the excuses not to get closer to nature, and replace them with these five reasons why you should pack your bags and experience the wonders of the earth:

1. With life pared to the essentials, we have the opportunity to rediscover and delight in the smallest things—too often taken for granted.

2. Being out with nature downsizes our preoccupation with our personal problems. Surrounded by the earth's vastness, we can't help but see that we're but very small creatures with a short time on earth. And if we're smart, we'll make that time count.

3. A nature experience provides a break in the action, disrupting our normal habits and forcing us to look beyond ourselves—opening the way for positive change.

4. Facing physical challenges gives us an opportunity to applaud our strengths as well as to work toward overcoming some of our weaknesses.

5. After an experience with nature, most people report an increased awareness, power, and sense of energy.[6]

Use the power of music and art to enhance your inner wholeness.

The ancient Greeks were the first who said that music could be used to heal. Aristotle believed the flute could arouse such strong emotions that it could lead to a cathartic release. Music was played with meals to aid digestion, at bedtime to induce sleep, any time to soothe the soul.[7] Art, too, has been used as a means to heal the human mind and body.

The way you respond to art and music is as personal as falling in love. You may be brought to tears by the intensity of voices in an Italian opera, while the person next to you dozes through the entire act. Maybe it's jazz that fills your soul. Or rock 'n roll. Perhaps impressionist paintings evoke an emotional response. Or the more daring work of Picasso . . . or Andy Warhol. Music and art speak a different language to each one of us. You may speak the language of color, or rhythm, or shapes, or melody. You may feel a spiritual connection when you create . . . or when you appreciate.

"Solitude is as needful to the imagination as society is wholesome for the character."
—James Russell Lowell

There's no prescription for discovering the magic. But here are a few suggestions from some whose appreciation of the arts has enriched their lives:

Go exploring. Treat yourself to a museum exhibit, concert, or dance performance. Push yourself to attend an art lecture or slide show. Be aware of what touches a chord. Do you feel tranquil in a

how come i feel so disconnected
if this is such a user-friendly world?

186

sculpture garden? Energized by a jazz festival? Stay receptive to any emotions evoked by your experiences.

Open the encyclopedia. Or get yourself a good biography. Read up on a composer or artist of your choice. Find out what was going on in his life when he created the masterpiece that moves you. Does the discovery add a new dimension to your appreciation of his works?

Use your friends. Take advantage of the people you know to share their knowledge, interests, and talents. See an art exhibit with a friend who's familiar with the artist's works and can help you better appreciate what you see. Make your opera debut with someone who can explain what's going on. Explore new avenues with those who can guide, teach, explain, demonstrate, and enrich your experience. Personal, artistic connections can sometimes be contagious.

Be daring—try something hands-on. Have you always wanted to take up a musical instrument? Do you still regret giving up piano lessons? Have you thought about taking a sketch pad outside and trying your hand? Does the idea of digging your fingers into a mound of clay excite you? Creative outlets have been found to be powerful enough to reverse negative forces and improve one's health. Self-expression has been touted as a stress reliever, ego gratifier, and source of pride and accomplishment.

When you find a source of connection, don't let it get away. Appreciate it. Enjoy it. Pursue it.

Feel better about yourself. Turn a weakness you thought was lifelong into a new-found strength.

We all have an Achilles' heel or two—those parts of ourselves that act as roadblocks, keeping us from happiness and success. Got a short temper? Worry too much? Maybe you're hypersensitive or chronically late. If you could change one thing to feel better about yourself, what would it be? The key to personal transformation is not to resist change, but to enjoy it. Our birthright is not to be invincible, but to learn, grow, and explore.

Sometimes even a minor change can have a major effect. Are you ready to take a good look at yourself? First, you need the right attitude. Repeat the following—until you believe:

1. I am bigger than my Achilles' heel. My weakness is not the sole measure of my self-worth.

2. I forgive myself for my Achilles' heel. I accept that nobody's perfect—not even me. The less harshly I judge myself, the more accepting I can become of others.

3. I can use my Achilles' heel. It can be an opportunity for growth and improvement. By addressing my weak spot, I can coach myself through change until I feel better about myself.

Once you've accepted your Achilles' heel and targeted the direction for change, let positive thinking be your guide.

> *"A man cannot be comfortable without his own approval."*
> —*Mark Twain*

Set your goal. "A self-destructive behavior I'm ready to give up is . . ." And for every small step you take, reward yourself. Pat yourself

how come i feel so disconnected
if this is such a user-friendly world?

188

on the back for every day without the negative behavior you're trying to change.

Reaffirm your goal. When you're guilty of the self-defeating trait or attitude, ask yourself:
- Did I gain anything from this?
- Did I lose anything?
- How did I feel when I did it?
- How did it affect others who were with me?
- Could I have handled this situation differently?
- Can I use my skills to transform my weakness into a source of strength?[8]

When you make progress, ask yourself the same questions. The more you like your answers, the better you'll feel about your behavior . . . and yourself.

Take inventory, and get rid of old commitments, chores, and habits that no longer quite fit.

Think about your clothes closet. You can't keep adding the new clothes you buy without now and then getting rid of what's already there. How rewarding it is to lighten and get rid of some clothes that after a while have become burdens. So, too, can old commitments and chores and old ways of doing things become burdens for us, weighing us down and holding us back, taking up valuable "room" in our selves.

But closets don't clean themselves. It's up to us to sort through our personal space in order to discover what's truly important. Without some reappraising and refocusing, it's not going to happen so fast. The ways we make room for change are not unfamiliar to any conscious person in the '90s.

• Reorder your priorities. If you put spending time with those closest to you further down your calendar of events because "they'll always be there," think again. They won't always—unless you will more often.

• Cast off extraneous obligations. If your 12-year-old book group has grown stale, if hosting the holidays every year is more work than fun, if chairing that committee is no longer a thrill—it's time to unburden yourself.

• If you walk around long enough believing that only you can be relied on to pick up the cleaning, send out birthday cards, or tape that TV show, soon you'll be right. Delegate—and free up some minutes to take a bath or listen to a song. Use those competent people around you as a team: a team who will profit from your spending more time with a person they admire and respect—you!

Appreciate. Enjoy. The only difference between optimists and pessimists is how they process the input they receive.

The more than 100 billion brain cells each of us possesses would need a computer 100 stories tall and the size of Texas to duplicate. The best skills this wondrous "computer" facilitates—insight, intuition, and inspiration—are seriously underutilized. Too many

how come i feel so disconnected
if this is such a user-friendly world?

190

brain cells are kept busy handling negative messages that emanate from the outside in. We have the ability, once we focus, to control the messages we give ourselves. Just as we can release the stress in our shoulders by simply being aware and letting it go, so too can we focus on peace of mind, harmony, success, and love . . . and find ourselves happier and more fulfilled.

Most of our resolutions are doomed to failure. We don't save enough, call our mothers enough, exercise enough, or eat enough fat-free stuff to satisfy our New Year's wish list.

What follows are some affirmations that just thinking can make so. The rewards will be greater and more long lasting than your vows to organize the family's photo album or straighten out the attic.

"I will pause more often and give myself the opportunity to experience the sensual ahs of our world." Part of the wonder of life is that each leaf, fruit, animal, or human being is distinctive. Through taking the time to appreciate the nuances of whatever food we eat, flower we smell, or person we encounter, we are connecting more strongly with the reasons we work so hard to survive.

"I will revise my definition of 'making it.'" "Happiness," said Benjamin Franklin, "is produced not so much by great pieces of good fortune that seldom happen as by the little advantages that occur every day." Life circumstances—even fame, unlimited leisure, and fortune—once we've adapted to them, bear little relation to our happiness. Satisfaction in life is less a matter of getting what we want than of wanting what we have.

"I will limit how far I allow myself to be seduced by technology." Allow time for your soul when you can't be phoned, faxed, or otherwise intruded on. Modern devices provide the opportunity for overworking—not a mandate. Ultraefficiency is only wonderful if the time saved is used for restorative relaxation.

"I will master the way I use my time." Set big goals, then break them down to daily projects. We tend to overestimate how much we can do in any given day and underestimate how much we can accomplish in a year. As each mini-deadline is met, we're rewarded with the unbeatable combined feeling of accomplishment and control.

"I will join the movement movement." For ages we've known it: a sound mind lives in a sound body. With a moderate commitment of time and minimal cost, we can almost guarantee that adding exercise to a sedentary life will boost energy, increase self-confidence, and decrease stress.

> *"The future belongs to those who believe in the beauty of their dreams."*
> —Eleanor Roosevelt

"I will believe that I already am where I wish to be." In experiments, people who feign high self-esteem soon begin feeling better about themselves. Even when manipulated into a smiling expression, people feel better. When they scowl, the whole world seems to scowl back. Pretend optimism. Simulate outgoingness. Going through the motions can trigger the emotions.

"I will live in the present because that's where I am." Too often we behave as if the present were merely our means to the future.

how come i feel so disconnected
if this is such a user-friendly world?

192

Happiness is not somewhere off in the future but lies in making our primary connecting points a priority.[9]

• CLOSING THOUGHTS

On a foggy morning some 45 years ago, 26 miles west of the California coastline, a 34-year-old woman dove into the water and began swimming the Catalina Channel toward the mainland. Her name was Florence Chadwick, and she had already been the first woman to swim the English Channel in both directions.

The water was numbing cold that morning, and the fog was so thick she could hardly see the boats in her own party. Millions were watching on television. Several times sharks had to be driven away with rifles. As the hours ticked off, Chadwick swam on.

More than 15 hours later, isolated and numb, she asked to be taken out. Her mother and her trainer, alongside in a boat, told her that she was near land. But when she looked toward the coast, all she could see was the dense fog.

Within the hour she quit. "Look," she said the next morning, "I'm not excusing myself, but if I could have seen the land, I might have made it."

She had been pulled out only half a mile from the California coast.

Later she reflected that it wasn't fatigue or the cold that defeated her, but the fog. With her goal obscured from sight, she couldn't go on.

Too many of us hustle through our lives, our way clouded by a thousand errands. The "shoulds" and "have tos" occupy time that would be better spent looking at the reality of where we are, what we are, and what we want to be. With our sense of self clouded, our goals remain hidden in the fog, and our behavior becomes disconnected and misdirected. We come to feel isolated, inadequate, and lost in the journey.

A stronger sense of self provides the opportunity to see beyond the fog: an opportunity to realistically look at—and assess—our place in the present relative to our lifetime goals. Then, with a greater clarity of vision, we can chart the course toward a more open and generous personal and familial future. With a clear picture of what is, we can create any tomorrow we choose.

(By the way, two months after her first attempt, Florence Chadwick swam the same channel, and again dense fog obscured her view. But this time she swam with her conviction intact—somewhere behind the fog was dry land. Not only was she the first woman to swim the Catalina Channel, but she beat the men's record by almost two hours!)

Endnotes

Although very little of our text was reprinted from other sources, many publications provided us with important information—and inspiration. These notes are our way of giving credit where credit is due—and to say "thank you" to these valuable resources.

CHAPTER ONE

1. Barry Wellman, Peter J. Carrington, and Alan Hall, "Networks as Personal Communities," *Social Structures: A Network Approach* (Cambridge: Cambridge University Press, 1988).
2. James R. Wetzel, "American Families: 75 Years of Change," *Monthly Labor Review,* March 1990.
3. Marcia Byalick and Linda Saslow, *The Three-Career Couple,* (Princeton: Peterson's, 1993).
4. Excerpted from the sermon of Rabbi Abner Bergman, delivered November 1992.

CHAPTER TWO

1. "Male Intimacy Report," Associated Press, *Newsday,* April 29, 1991.
2. Ibid.
3. Elizabeth Wood and Floris Wood, *She Said, He Said* (Michigan: Visible Ink Press, 1992).
4. Harold Bloomfield, Sarah Veteese, and Robert Kory, "Tapping the Power of Intimacy," *Prevention,* October 1990.
5. "Secrets of Successful Families: Exclusive Survey," *Family Circle,* November 23, 1993.

how come i feel so disconnected
if this is such a user-friendly world?

196

6. Frank Pittman, *Private Lives: Infidelity and the Betrayal of Intimacy* (New York: Norton, 1989).

7. Anne Slavicek, "Good Marriages Hinged on Friendship, Seniors Say," *San Diego Woman,* July 1988.

8. Ibid.

9. Michael S. Broder, *The Art of Staying Together: A Couples' Guide to Intimacy and Respect* (New York: Hyperion, 1993).

10. Pamela Adelmann, "Marital Myths: What We 'Know' Hurts," *Psychology Today,* May 1989.

11. Ronald Smothers, "Tell It to Mom, Dad and the Authorities," *New York Times,* November 13, 1993.

12. Katherine Barrett and Richard Greene, "Video: The New Family Fix," *Ladies' Home Journal,* February 1990.

13. "More Health, Sex Classes Urged," *Newsday,* November 29, 1993.

14. William J. Doherty, "Private Lives, Public Values," *Psychology Today,* June 1992.

15. Elizabeth Wood and Floris Wood, op. cit.

16. Ibid.

17. Ibid.

18. Marcia Byalick and Linda Saslow, *The Three-Career Couple,* (Princeton: Peterson's, 1993).

19. Beth Sherman, "The Dirt on Men," *Newsday,* September 26, 1992.

20. Sally Wendkos Olds, *The Working Parents' Survival Guide,* (Rocklin, CA: Prima Publishing and Communications, 1989).

21. Elizabeth Wood and Floris Wood, op. cit.

22. *New York Motorist,* May 1994.

23. "An Insider's Guide to Teen Speak," *Reader's Digest,* May 1992.

CHAPTER THREE

1. *Bottom Line,* August 16, 1993.

2. Elizabeth Wood and Floris Wood, *She Said, He Said,* (Michigan: Visible Ink Press, 1992).

3. Lynn White, "Social Forces," University of North Carolina Press, 1994.

4. Ellen Goodman, "You Can't Teleconference Thanksgiving," *Newsday,* November 23, 1994.

5. Jane Mersky Leder, "Adult Sibling Rivalry," *Psychology Today,* January/February 1993.

6. Lynn White, op. cit.

7. Jane Mersky Leder, op. cit.

8. Lynn White, op. cit.

9. Ibid.

10. Jane Mersky Leder, op. cit.

11. Elizabeth Stone, "Friends Again: When Sisters Become Moms," *Parents,* April 1992.

12. Marilyn Mayo, "Tracing Family Roots," *Parents,* June 1992; Anne Sylvester, "Tracing Your Roots," *Cosmopolitan,* November 1989; "Facts About Family Trees," *Woman's Day,* March 24, 1987.

13. Ann Sylvester, op. cit.; Marilyn Mayo, op. cit.

14. Maymie R. Krythe, *All About American Holidays* (New York: Harper, 1962).

15. Evan Imber-Black and Janine Roberts, "Family Change: Don't Cancel Holidays!" *Psychology Today,* March/April 1993.

16. Milbry Polk, "How to Organize a Family Reunion," *Americana,* March 1992.

CHAPTER FOUR

1. Harry Reis and Peter Franks, "The Role of Intimacy and Social Support in Health Outcomes: Two Processes or One?" University of Rochester, 1993.

how come i feel so disconnected
if this is such a user-friendly world?

198

2. Eugene Kennedy, *On Being a Friend* (New York: Continuum, 1982).

3. Kate Meyers, "Scoring Points for Love," *Health,* March 1990.

4. Alessandra Bianchi, "Contemporary Greetings," *Inc.,* January 1994

5. "Sending Your Very Best," *Psychology Today,* November/December 1992.

6. Ibid.

7. "The Relationship Is in the Mail," *Harper's,* May 1991.

8. Letty Cottin Pogrebin, *Among Friends* (New York: McGraw Hill, 1987).

9. Alan Loy McGinnis, *The Friendship Factor* (Minneapolis: Augsburg, 1979).

10. Ibid.

11. Steven Duck, *Friends for Life: The Psychology of Close Relationships* (New York: St. Martin's, 1991).

CHAPTER FIVE

1. Barry Wellman, Peter J. Carrington, and Alan Hall, "Networks as Personal Communities," *Social Structures: A Network Approach* (Cambridge: Cambridge University Press, 1988).

2. Karen E. Campbell, "Networks Past: 1939 Bloomington Neighborhood," University of North Carolina Press, September 1990.

3. Bonni Marlewski-Probert, "Tips for Starting a Neighborhood Watch," *Good Housekeeping,* October 1993.

4. Ibid.

5. David E. Driver, *The Good Heart Book: A Guide to Volunteering* (Chicago: Noble, 1989).

6. Steven L. Nock, *The Cost of Privacy: Surveillance and Reputation in America* (New York: Aldine de Gruyter, 1993).

7. Phone interview with Al Splete, President of the Council of Independent Colleges, Washington, D.C.

8. Alan Luks and Peggy Payne, *The Healing Power of Doing Good* (New York: Fawcett Columbine, 1991).

9. Thomas Quick, *Successful Team Building* (AMA Worksmart Service, 1992).

CHAPTER SIX

1. Kenneth L. Woodward, "Talking to God," *Newsweek,* January 6, 1992.

2. Kenneth L. Woodward, "Why America Prays," *Newsweek,* January 6, 1992.

3. Ibid.

4. Cathy Benson, "Pray for Peace," *Prevention,* June 1991.

5. Mary Nemeth and Nora Underwood, "God Is Alive," *Macleans,* April 1993.

6. Susan Chira, "Generation That Left Church Goes Back with Its Children," *New York Times,* December 26, 1993.

7. Marc Gellman and Thomas Hartman, *Where Does God Live?* (New York: Triumph Books, 1991).

8. Marlise Simons, "Pilgrims Crowding Europe's Catholic Shrines," *New York Times,* October 12, 1993.

9. Marsha G. Witten, *All Is Forgiven* (Princeton: Princeton University Press, 1993).

10. "The National Survey of Religious Identification," *Christianity Today,* May 27, 1991.

11. "Future of Mainline Religion, Social Science and Citizen," *Society,* March/April, 1992.

12. Elizabeth Wood and Floris Wood, *She Said, He Said* (Michigan: Visible Ink Press, 1992).

13. William Hendricks, "What's Wrong with This Picture?" *Christianity Today,* November 1991.

14. Leonard R. N. Ashley, *What's In a Name?* (Baltimore: Genealogical Publishing, 1989).

how come i feel so disconnected
if this is such a user-friendly world?

200

CHAPTER SEVEN

1. Gail Collins, "Why No One Wants to Work Anymore," *Working Woman,* May 1993.

2. Ibid.

3. "Shortcuts," *Newsday,* September 9, 1994.

4. "American Business 2000," *Fortune,* June 23, 1992.

5. Barbara Presley Noble, "The Debate Over La Difference," *New York Times,* August 15, 1993.

6. Robert B. Reich, "Companies Are Cutting Their Hearts Out," *New York Times Magazine,* December 19, 1993.

7. "Have a Nice Day: Employee Loyalty in Service Firms," *Economist,* March 2, 1991.

8. "Married to the Job," *Psychology Today,* July/August 1992.

9. "Bottom Line: Wandering Bosses," *Newsday,* November 23, 1993.

10. Barbara Presley Noble, "We're Doing Just Fine, Thank You," *New York Times,* March 20, 1994.

11. Jon Robert Steinberg, "The Forty-Five-Plus Generation," *New Choices,* January 1991.

12. "The Death of Corporate Loyalty," *Economist,* April 3, 1993.

13. Barbara Presley Noble, "Of Bosses, Barriers and Beliefs," *New York Times,* March 6, 1994.

14. "American Business 2000," op. cit.

15. Alistair Bonnett, "Stealing Our Lives," *New Statesman and Society,* November 22, 1992.

16. *Family Circle* Survey, November 23, 1993.

17. "What High Achieving Career Women Say," *Newsday,* October 3, 1993.

18. Marian Sandmaier, "Why Flattering the Boss Works Better for Men," *Working Woman,* October 1991.

19. Laura Muha, "Study: Older Workers a Good Value," *Newsday,* November 22, 1993.

20. Robin Schatz, "It's Satisfaction as Much as Cash," *Newsday,* September 3, 1993.

21. *The National Study of the Changing Workforce* (New York: Families and Work Institute, 1993).

22. Ibid.

23. Robert Levering, *A Great Place to Work* (New York: Random House, 1988).

24. *The National Study of the Changing Workforce,* op. cit.

25. Stephen Strasser and John Sena, *Work Is Not a Four-Letter Word* (Illinois: Business One Irwin, 1992).

26. "Are We Having Fun Yet?" *Industry Week,* March 4, 1991.

27. Nancy Marx Better, "Learning to Handle Anger at Work," *Self,* June 1992.

28. Tony Alessandra and Phil Hunsaker, *Communication at Work* (New York: Simon and Schuster, 1993).

29. Madelyn Burley-Allen, *Managing Assertively* (New York: John Wiley & Sons, 1983).

30. Harvey Gittler, "Give Yourself a Present," *Industry Week,* December 1993.

31. Alice Bredin, "Job, Sweet Job," *Newsday,* September 13, 1993.

CHAPTER EIGHT

1. Natalie Goldberg, *Writing Down the Bones* (Boston: Shambhala, 1986).

2. Andrew Weill, "What Is Holistic Health?" *Holistic Health Directory and Resource Guide, 1994–5.*

3. Interview with Steven Schenkman, president of the New Center for Wholistic Health, Education, and Research, Syosset, New York.

how come i feel so disconnected
if this is such a user-friendly world?

202

4. Dwight Holing, *A Guide to Earth Trips* (Los Angeles: Conservation International Living Planet Press, 1991).

5. Ibid.

6. Ibid.; Daniel Goleman, "Psychology's New Interest in the World Beyond the Self," *New York Times,* November 14, 1993.

7. Kay Gardner, "Music as Medicine," *Ms.,* July/August 1991.

8. Joyce Brothers, "Some Techniques That Can Help You Turn a Drawback into a Strength," *Parade,* April 10, 1994.

9. Stephen M. Pollan and Mark Levine, "The Graying Yuppie," *New York,* March 9, 1992.